"For 29 years I went Park two to three times per week as the Medical Officer. I always stopped to chat with the commissionaires and with one in particular, Bruce Menzies. Bruce told me several of his stories about HMCS *Waskesiu*. The ship's crew braved the North Atlantic in the worst weather and always with the threat of a U-boat attack. Their reward for doing this—turn around and do it all again. The frigates and corvettes in the end won the 'Battle of the Atlantic'. As a Cold War sailor, my heroes were the men who manned the RCN ships in World War Two—and what a great shipmate Bruce Menzies would have made. Bravo Zulu to all who sailed in HMCS *Waskesiu*."

—Commander John Blatherwick,
  CM, CstJ, OBC, CD, MD, FRCP(C), LLD;
  Principal Medical Officer (Ret'd), HMCS *Discovery*;
  Chief Medical Health Officer (Ret'd), City of Vancouver

"We of today's Navy can only read about and imagine the shipboard conditions endured by those hardy men on the WWII Murmansk Run, whose survival is a testament to their courage and personal strength of character. I consider it a great honour to know Bruce Menzies, who for many years has been proudly regaling our sailors with his stories, instilling in this generation a respect and admiration for all who served before them. To those who made the greatest sacrifice, I offer a salute, in the naval tradition, to 'Absent Friends'."

—Lieutenant-Commander Elaine Fisher, CD;
  Commanding Officer, HMCS *Discovery*

WASKESIU

Canada's First Frigate

R. L. Duane Duff

DUFF
PUBLISHING
.CA

Surrey, British Columbia, Canada

Editor, designer: Sean G. Duff

Printed in the United States of America

Library and Archives Canada Cataloguing in Publication

Duff, R. L. Duane, 1930-
　　　Waskesiu : Canada's first frigate / R.L. Duane Duff.

Includes bibliographical references.
ISBN 978-0-9810784-3-4

　　　1. Waskesiu (Ship). 2. World War, 1939-1945--Naval operations, Canadian. 3. Canada. Royal Canadian Navy--Biography. 4. Sailors--Canada--Biography. 5. World War, 1939-1945--Personal narratives, Canadian. 6. Veterans--Canada--Biography. I. Title.

VA400.5.W38D83 2008　　　940.54'5971　　　C2008-907167-0

Duff Publishing
13866 60 Avenue
Surrey, BC V3X 2N1
Canada
www.duffpublishing.ca

In memory of the veterans of
HMCS *Waskesiu*

WASKESIU: Canada's First Frigate

It is the VETERAN, not the preacher,
who has given us freedom of religion.

It is the VETERAN, not the reporter,
who has given us freedom of the press.

It is the VETERAN, not the poet,
who has given us freedom of speech.

It is the VETERAN, not the campus organizer,
who has given us freedom to assemble.

It is the VETERAN, not the lawyer,
who has given us the right to a fair trial.

It is the VETERAN, not the politician,
who has given us the right to vote.

It is the VETERAN,
who salutes the flag.

It is the VETERAN,
who serves under the flag.

—*Author unknown*

WASKESIU: Canada's First Frigate

Contents

Foreword

The Royal Canadian Navy contributed a major share to the overall victory in the Battle of the Atlantic against Hitler. HMCS *Waskesiu* and her crew can be proud of their record as part of a major naval force that defended against coastal and convoy threats from German U-boats.

This book includes delightful and factual anecdotes from veterans who relate in their own words the experience of joining the *Waskesiu* while most were in their late teens and enduring both the hardship and adventure of life at sea in the North Atlantic. The book will rekindle emotions and images of such unimaginable incidents as their sister convoy patrol ship being torpedoed and sinking before their very eyes. The crew are all heroes who deserve to have their stories documented and shared with fellow Canadians.

It was because of a chance meeting between Duane Duff and Bruce Menzies, a *Waskesiu* veteran, who used his persuasive powers on the author that this book be written.

The German officer who survived the U-257 sinking and became good friends with the *Waskesiu* veterans is a very touching part of the book. The book could have been entitled, "When Enemies Become Friends".

Waskesiu's contribution to the war at sea was a proud achievement and is a record of loyalty and faithful service which we hope will not be forgotten by succeeding generations.

Capt.(N)(R) Don Ravis (Ret'd)
October 2008

Don Ravis was a member of the Naval Reserve for twenty-seven years and retired as Commanding Officer of HMCS *Unicorn* in Saskatoon. He served as a Member of Parliament during 1984–1988. He is a seasonal resident at Waskesiu Lake in Prince Albert National Park and is currently Chair of the Waskesiu Community Council.

Preface

One day, our family took our former colleagues from Alberta—Art and Suzan Horovitch, of Montreal—to visit Stanley Park, in Vancouver. As we walked past the gate house at HMCS *Discovery*, Art decided to stop.

Bruce Menzies, a commissionaire, was on duty. As soon as they learned that each had Montreal roots, they engaged in conversation. I walked over to join them.

After a time, I sensed a story for an upcoming book, and Bruce was quite willing to accept my offer. We parted company with my promise to contact him at a later date and bring my portable tape recorder. He and his colleagues had long been hoping to find someone to write a history of their ship.

A couple of months later, my wife Pam and I kept the appointment that I made with Bruce a few days earlier. Part way through the interview, Pam became aware that I was receiving more than I needed for a chapter in my book. Then, Bruce stated his desire that my book should be about HMCS *Waskesiu*.

It took me a while to recognize the enormity of my task to which I was being drafted; however, I accepted the challenge. Bruce gave me much information, including the list of surviving members with contact information, from which I was to begin the work.

I sent a questionnaire to each of the veterans for basic information while Bruce contacted them to encourage them to send me their questionnaires fully answered. After I had received these and recorded them, I telephoned each with further questions. These conversations were taped and then transcribed.

All of these men were very cooperative and encouraging. One survivor, who lives in the same city as I do, brought his data to me. We had an enjoyable visit that day.

Bruce visited me, bringing me more information, and he telephoned me to follow my progress and to provide any news that he had gathered. He is to be commended for his  persistence in trying to have a book written about HMCS *Waskesiu*. Without his efforts and his assistance, this book could not have been completed.

I am honoured to have been requested to compile this book, which I hope will provide the reader with interesting information about the ship and its crew. We can appreciate what these former sailors and others did at the risk of their lives to help to defend our country and the people of the world.

Acknowledgments

Bruce Menzies and I thank Derek Richer, a commercial writer in Vancouver, and Dorell Taylor, editor of *Waskesiu Memories*, who have made significant contributions to keep the story of HMCS *Waskesiu* alive. Some of the work of both writers has been used within this book. Beyond their work, so little of a lasting nature has been written about the ship and its accomplishments.

Robert Banks, an artist from North Vancouver, provided us with a copy of a painting of HMCS *Waskesiu*. Bo Hermanson, member of the Canadian Society of Marine Artists in Victoria, provided us with a copy of a painting of the battle between HMCS *Waskesiu* and U-257. Permission to use both these paintings is much appreciated.

We thank Walter Ritchie, who was granted permission from the captain to have a camera on board, for allowing us to include many of those pictures that he took of the ship and crew during active service.

Roland Berr, from Geisenfeld, Bavaria, Germany, provided a picture and data about U-257. Hubertus Weggelaar, from Australind, Western Australia, provided a crew list.

A few of the veterans checked the content of this book for accuracy of information. Alejandro Duff, our grandson, took photographs. Art and Suzan Horovitch, of Montreal, assisted with the proofreading. Sean Duff has done all the work in editing, layout, and publishing.

The following persons have also helped us in some way to obtain the data necessary to compile this book. To each, we extend our thanks.

From Ottawa: Lt.-Cdr. Graeme Arbuckle, Navy Heritage Officer, Directorate of History and Heritage; Lt.-Cdr. Sue Stefko, Navy Public Affairs; and S. Dumas, Veterans Affairs Canada.

From Victoria: Lt. Karl Hoener, communications officer, Naden Wardroom, CFB Esquimalt; and Ruth A. Scott, branch head, Esquimalt Branch Library.

From Saskatchewan: Ione Langlois, curator, Waskesiu Heritage Museum; Bob Twyver, administrator, Waskesiu Community Council; Dr. Bill Waiser, Department of History, University of Saskatchewan; and Mickey Zwack, Prince Albert *Daily Herald*.

From India: Admiral Madhvendra Singh, Ministry of Defence (Navy), New Delhi; Jagmal Singh, assistant library and information officer, National Library of India, Kolkata; and Shashi U Tripathi, High Commissioner for India in Ottawa.

From Germany: Timo Cernohorsky, translator, Schwaebisch Hall, Baden-Wuerttemberg.

And a special thank you to the surviving members of HMCS *Waskesiu* for sharing their time, material, and recollections of their experiences aboard Canada's first frigate.

Introduction

Before anyone on the three warships could react, three torpedoes had been launched from the German submarine. One passed off the bow of HMCS *Waskesiu*; however, it was on target with HMS *Tweed*. What followed was tragic. *Waskesiu*, on her first big mission in the North Atlantic Ocean off the coasts of Europe and Africa, just had her baptism into anti-submarine warfare.

In an early morning search for an elusive submarine, star shells and flares lit up the moonless sky and the dark choppy sea. The noise of the ASDIC instrument was unnerving to the operators as the frigate closed in on the submarine. Meanwhile, the exploding depth charges made life unbearable in the submarine beneath the murky waves.

The crew experienced the cold and danger of running the gauntlet from the United Kingdom to the Arctic coast of Russia. This was a lifeline for the Russians as freighters brought needed supplies to an ally. *Waskesiu* and other warships from various countries had the unenviable task of defending the freighters laden with their precious cargo. Who would like crow's nest duty in the Arctic?

At night, the German submarines infested the cold waters. In the daytime, the German dive bombers swarmed in the sky. The enemy did have a measure of success, but not total by any means. The crew of *Waskesiu* grumbled about setting out the cat gear, but changed their attitude when they witnessed what it did for them on one particular occasion.

What do you do when you are refueling at sea and you see a torpedo skimming along the surface of the water, making a beeline between the two ships? Aircraft carrier HMS *Vindex* and frigate HMCS *Waskesiu* witnessed this potential disaster unfolding. The crews knew their jobs and responded promptly.

When the long-awaited invasion of Europe had arrived, *Waskesiu* was one of hundreds of ships participating. Even though she was on the periphery of the action, it was not quiet. It was like May 24 to one crew member on *Waskesiu* as he watched the sky light up. The depth charges exterminated more fish than enemy submarines. It was a horrendous experience seeing in the rough water the many soldiers and airmen who had died from enemy fire.

Not all of their time during the war was at action stations. There were exciting leaves in Ireland, Scotland, and England. There were the church services for which the sailors had differing opinions. What do you think of using a gun to bring on board mail from home? Doing duty watch on board was easy or unpleasant, depending on your orders. Sleeping in hammocks in the mess hall was normal. Watching one's utensils slip across the table at meal time created deftness in corralling one's food. Having to prepare hardtack for dinner was a challenge for a cook when supplies ran low.

A few of the veterans mull over their past. Would they have traded the experience for something else? A reunion of old sea hands after more than five decades is a sight to behold. Add to that the presence of a former enemy who became a close friend. These men have many memories and, with excitement, share some of them here.

The reader will come to comprehend what these hardy souls accomplished for our country at risk to their own lives.

A glossary of 150 entries is available near the back to aid the reader in understanding the acronyms, slang, and general naval terminology used frequently throughout the book.

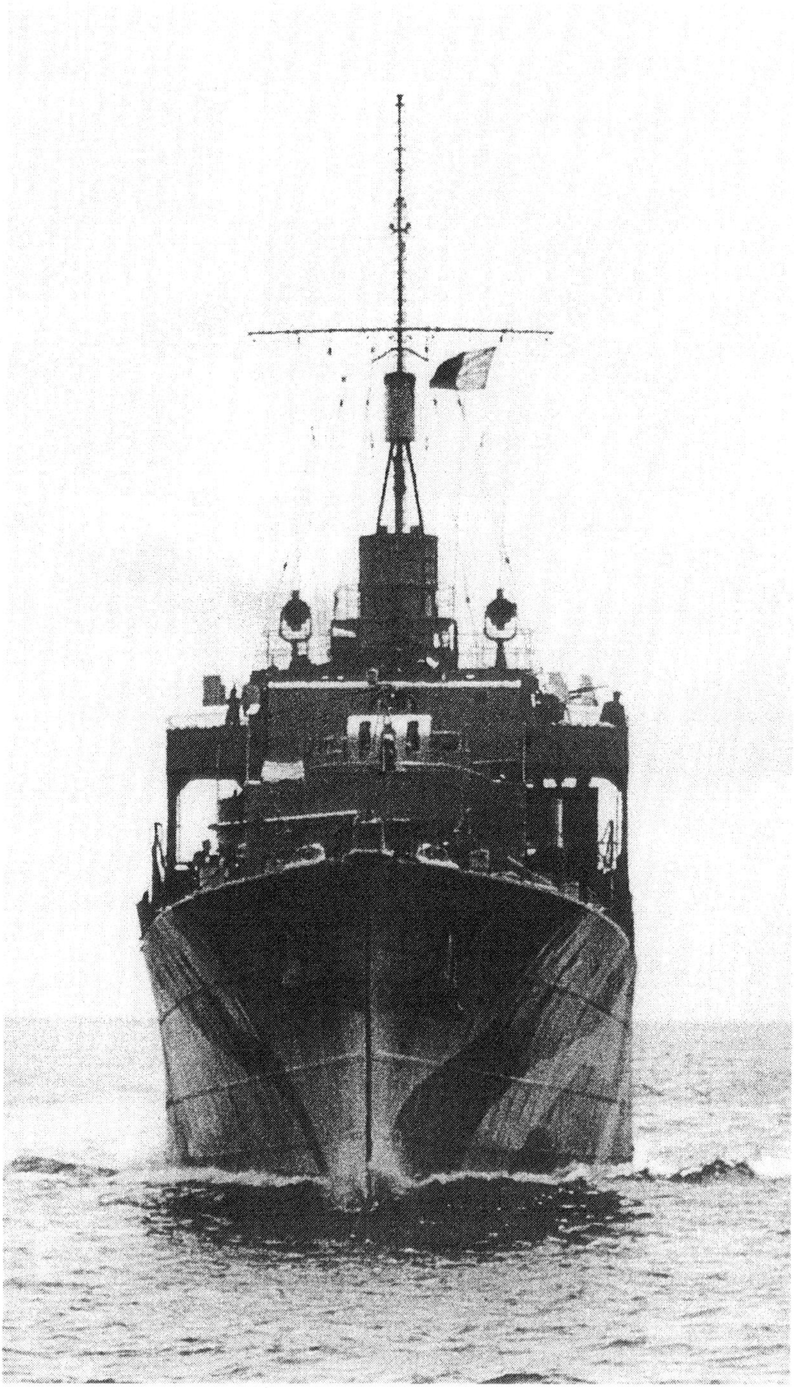

1

Rebirth of the Frigates

HMCS *Waskesiu* was the first of sixty frigates completed on the west coast of Canada for the Royal Canadian Navy. She was laid down on May 2, 1942; launched on April 3, 1943; and commissioned at Yarrows Shipyard in Esquimalt, BC, on June 16, 1943.

She was named for Prince Albert, Saskatchewan. Since that name was taken by a ship of the Royal Navy, HMS *Prince Albert* (1864-1899), she was given the name *Waskesiu*, that of a townsite located in Prince Albert National Park. Other names were also considered.

The *River* class frigate, HMCS *Waskesiu* being one, was a class of 151 frigates launched between 1941 and 1944 for use as anti-submarine convoy escorts in the North Atlantic.

It was redesigned from the original corvette by naval engineer William Reed to have the endurance and anti-submarine capabilities of the *Black Swan* class sloops, while being quick and inexpensive to build in civil dockyards using the machinery (e.g., reciprocating steam engines instead of turbines) and construction techniques pioneered in the building of the *Flower* class corvettes.

All Royal Navy frigates were named for rivers and, hence, were known as *River* class.

The name "frigate" was adopted at the suggestion of Vice-Admiral Percy Nelles, Canada's Chief of Naval Staff. The term was first used for ships in war by the Portuguese in the sixteenth and seventeenth centuries. Later, the French and British adopted it to designate a definite class of warships—ships next in class to ships of the line. The name has now been revived by the Canadian Navy.

The majority served with the Royal Navy and Royal Canadian Navy, with some serving in the other Allied navies. After World War II they found employment in many other navies around the world; however, several RCN ships were sunk as breakwaters.

This new class of anti-submarine escort ship represented a major advance over the corvettes in speed (by three or four knots); ASDIC capability, with the most modern set coupled to the type 147 depth predictor set; and a half times the number of depth charges.

While the corvettes and the hard-worn destroyers had led the way during the early and desperate convoy battles, these frigates and the Squid-equipped *Castle* class corvettes effectively ended the hopes of *Grossadmiral* Karl Dönitz for at least a stalemate with the new class of U-boats and their increased effectiveness and weapons.

These frigates could remain away from their convoy while hunting U-boats and yet catch up again unlike the corvettes that, on occasion, were left far behind for days, or had to give up even promising hunts in order to regain their visual station with a convoy.

As well, the numbers of the new frigates in late 1943 and 1944 allowed for the formation of roving support groups subordinate to the close escorts because of their speed, weaponry, and flexibility to hunt submarines to exhaustion.

The new generation of U-boats would have posed a serious problem even for these ships, but they were too few and too late.

The frigates were faster, bigger, more sea-worthy, and better equipped than the corvettes, which were designed for coastal work only. They were the first Canadian-built warships to be fitted with the 147B "Sword" protruding below the hull to determine the depth of underwater targets by a horizontal fan of transmissions and returning echoes. The regular ASDIC obtained the range and bearing of the targets by using a similar, but vertical, fan.

Because they were too long to manipulate the St. Lawrence canal system, frigates could not be built along the Great Lakes as some other warships were. Therefore, all Canadian frigates were built on the west coast or St. Lawrence River yards. They were named for Canadian cities and towns.

The land for the Yarrow Shipyards was first established as a shipyard by the Bullen brothers in

1893, and then in 1914 sold to Sir Alfred Yarrow, who appointed his son, Norman Yarrow, to the presidency of the new establishment.

Many warships, including twenty-two ships of the Royal Canadian Navy, were built and refitted in this yard. Yarrows also worked on non-military projects, including work for the Canadian National Steamship and BC Ferries. Norman Yarrow managed his yard until the end of World War II and sold it in 1946.

2

Ocean to Ocean

On July 8, 1943, three weeks after being commissioned, *Waskesiu* left Victoria bound for Halifax to begin her exciting mission. Along the way, there were a few stops.

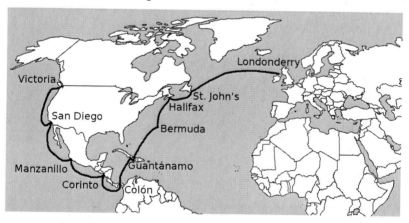

The first stop was at San Diego, California, where some of the fellows took a shore leave and went to Los Angeles. Charlie Robinson remembered having danced with Shirley Temple at the Hollywood Canteen. Highlights for Walter Ritchie were meeting such Hollywood stars as Deanna Durbin and Gracie Fields and attending a radio show featuring Harry James and his band.

On July 22, the warship stopped briefly at Manzanillo, Mexico. The men felt that this was a dirty town in appearance. Since there was no fresh water there, it had to be brought in by rail.

Five days later, she was in Corinto, Nicaragua. By now, everyone was in the white tropical uniforms. From there, she proceeded to Panama and the Panama Canal. At the Caribbean end of the canal, she stopped at Colón. She stayed here from August 2 to August 8 to allow for degaussing and other equipment upgrades.

Degaussing was a means to try to counter the German magnetic mines that were playing havoc with the British fleet. The mines detected the increase in magnetic field when the steel in a ship concentrated Earth's magnetic field over it. All clocks and electrical equipment were removed from the ship during the procedure.

On August 11, *Waskesiu* arrived in Guantánamo, Cuba, where she took on fuel oil. However, as the gangway was being lowered, two-inch (5-cm) cockroaches began to ascend it. Seeing that, the men immediately dropped the gang plank into the sea. The ship moved out of the harbour, where the anchor was dropped. The men went ashore by means of a motor launch.

From Cuba, she sailed to Bermuda, where she stayed from August 15 to September 8. Here the sailors obtained their training, known as evolutions, as a new ship's crew. Since this was a British naval base, the instructors were members of the Royal Navy.

The Canadians enjoyed taking this training in a tropical climate. Some of the training involved submarine chasing and jumping with life jackets on over the side of their ship into the tropical water. The men could not use the heads on board because of the clear water and tropical fish near the jetty. They had to use the facilities ashore at the jetty.

When the work had been completed, *Waskesiu* sailed for Halifax. Charlie Robinson remembered the date as being September 8, 1943, the day that Italy surrendered. Some sailors discovered that their tropical uniforms were not suitable for the harsh cold of Nova Scotia.

On September 11, the ship left Halifax. Now being in the North Atlantic, the sailors kept their life jacket at hand at all times because of the risks. On September 26, there was a stop-over at St. John's, Newfoundland.

The trip to Londonderry, Northern Ireland, was uneventful, with the arrival being on November 1.

Then on November 13, *Waskesiu's* assignment of searching for anything dangerous to the Allied shipping commenced, accompanied by HMS *Nene*.

Specifications for HMCS *Waskesiu*

Type: Frigate, *River* class
Pennant No.: K330
Ordered: 10 JUN 1941
Laid down: 2 MAY 1942
Launched: 3 APR 1943
Commissioned: 16 JUN 1943
Paid Off: 29 JAN 1946
Displacement: 1,445 tonnes
Length: 301 feet 6 inches (91.90 m)
Breadth: 36 feet 7 inches (11.15 m)
Depth (draught): 9 feet (2.74 m)

Crew: 12 officers, 133 other ranks

Speed: 19 knots (22 mph, 35 km/h)

Operating Radius: 9,500 miles (15,300 km) at 10–12 knots

Power Source: 2 Admiralty three-drum boilers and reciprocating Parsons SR geared turbines, twin screws

Armament: 1 four-inch (10-cm) gun forward, twin 20-mm (8-in) AA mounts in a sponson aft of the funnel, 4 depth charge throwers, twin DC traps in the stern, 150–200 depth charges, Hedgehog spigot mortar mounted on forecastle.

3

Tweed Sinks

E arly in 1944, HMCS *Waskesiu* and HMS *Nene* were supporting convoys running to Gibraltar and Sierra Leone.

On January 7, the two warships were working with HMS *Tweed* near the Azores. A bomber on patrol had sighted a German U-boat prior to the previous midnight. The three frigates searched for the submarine until 10:00 AM. Then the CO aboard *Nene* called off the search.

At 4:00 PM, the three ships were sailing abreast two miles apart on a zigzagging course, with *Nene* in the

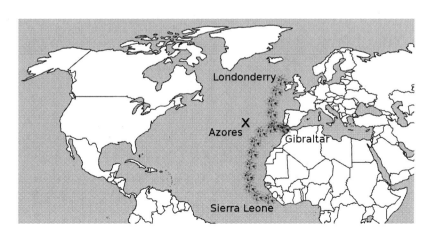

centre, *Tweed* on the port side, and *Waskesiu* on the starboard side—all travelling at about 15 knots (17 mph, 28 km/h).

On viewing through the periscope, *Kapitanleutnant* Rudolph Bahr, captain of U-305, saw the escorts at about 5,000 metres (3 mi). Ah! There are three targets for the picking. When ASDIC "pings" were heard on the hull, the captain ordered three torpedoes launched. The ASDIC operators on *Tweed* reported another contact at the same time. It was too late!

The dramatic part was the timing of the event. Prior to this, they were three ships abreast, with *Tweed* on the starboard position, *Nene* in the centre, and *Waskesiu* on the port side. However, at 4:00 PM, the command from *Nene* ordered *Tweed* and *Waskesiu* to exchange positions. Ten minutes later, in its new position, *Tweed* was torpedoed!

Tweed was about to execute a starboard zigzag when the ASDIC hut reported a submarine contact. The alarm bells sounded "A/S stations", which was immediately followed by the torpedo hit.

As water poured into the magazine, Lt.-Cdr. R. S. Miller gave the order to abandon ship. The ship sank in fifteen minutes or less, too quickly to launch a life-boat, and carried many sailors down with it. Some on the deck of *Waskesiu* witnessed the hit and the quick sinking of *Tweed*. It was a harrowing experience.

At the submersion point of *Tweed*, there were survivors, dead bodies, and wreckage on the oily water. As those who were able to escape were swimming away from the ship, two depth charges exploded nearby. This was responsible for all the casualties which occurred in the water.

Nene commander John Birch ordered his ship and *Waskesiu* to cut their speed. Everyone was on edge because of the threat of torpedoes. The two ships were in danger as long as they could not locate the submarine. Only once did the crews see the periscope—only briefly.

When *Waskesiu* left to track the submarine as ordered, *Tweed's* sailors in the water felt as though they were being abandoned and were very unhappy. They could not understand! Gordon Arnold will never forget their cries for help.

Survivors from *Tweed* grabbed hold of any debris that floated, eventually being rescued by HMS *Nene*. While *Nene* searched for survivors, *Waskesiu* continued the ASDIC sweep for the elusive submarine. Since she had made contact, she could not help in the rescue.

Depth charges were being dropped. After a time, *Waskesiu* joined in the search for U-305, while changing course and speed constantly in order to avoid acoustic torpedoes.

George Devonshire was concerned when one of the Hedgehog attacks came near to the survivors in the water and he could not help them. For Andy Kaija, it was the only time that he really felt a little apprehensive aboard *Waskesiu*.

The crew of U-305 heard the blast, and apparently escaped. (It was sunk several days later by a pair of HMS

destroyers.) Because of all the oil on the water, the crew of *Waskesiu* did not know whether the submarine had been hit and sunk or had actually escaped.

When contact was lost, the two frigates returned to the rescuing of survivors. They were able to save forty-eight ratings, the CO, and seven other officers. However, the next morning, January 8, five of them had died and were buried at sea at dawn.

On the following morning, *Nene* proceeded to Londonderry with the survivors from *Tweed*. Commander Birch came on board *Waskesiu* from *Nene* to command the operations. Now, *Waskesiu* was patrolling without the help of another ship.

On January 10, the ASDIC crew reported contacts. At this time, the crew had need of sleep. Besides that, Gordon Arnold reported that provisions were running low. One day later, *Waskesiu* joined another convoy and took on oil from a tanker. A submarine was seen briefly, but it disappeared.

On January 12, she joined another convoy which had reported U-boat sightings. By this time, the crew was down to hardtack. Canned milk, fresh vegetables, and potatoes were depleted. It was now powdered milk and dehydrated potatoes. When they ran out of salt on the next day, they resorted to salt from seawater to use at the table.

On January 15, *Nene* rejoined the convoy and Commander Birch and his staff returned to her one day later. Gordon Arnold, in charge of rations, was particularly happy that *Nene* brought back flour, salt, and canned milk for five more days.

Over the next few days, *Waskesiu* joined two other convoys briefly. By January 21, the food supplies were practically gone. Thus, permission was asked to proceed for supplies.

On February 5, their commanding officer, Lt.-Cdr. J. S. H. MacDonald, was reassigned. Lt.-Cdr. James P. Fraser assumed duties as the new CO. The men spoke highly of their departing captain.

4

Battle with the U-Boat

It was February 24, 1944, a dark night, and HMCS *Waskesiu* was on the seventeenth day out from Londonderry on her anti-submarine run in the mid Atlantic Ocean. Her captain, Lt.-Cdr. James Fraser, had been in command for only two days.

Shortly after 2:00 AM, the ASDIC crew picked up a possible submarine contact. German submarine U-257 had surfaced to send a message and to receive a weather report. *Waskesiu* locked onto the submarine and began tracking it.

The commanding officer ordered a Hedgehog attack—little torpedoes that were dispatched twenty-five at a time and exploded almost simultaneously once one of them hit something—but they missed their target. A flare was dropped over the stern of the ship. ASDIC contact had been lost.

Waskesiu turned about and returned to the spot where contact had previously been made and dropped a depth charge. At 2:26 AM, the captain ordered a full pattern depth charge attack. This rocked the submarine.

When the submarine went out of range, it was necessary for the frigate to turn around and try again. If the submarine did not eventually surface after a battle, it was assumed that it had gone to the bottom of the ocean.

Everyone on board *Waskesiu*, according to his position, was glued on the spot where the crew presumed that the submarine was lurking beneath the surface.

When Bruce Menzies, one of the ASDIC operators, picked up contact with the submarine, excitement and fear ran through the crew. Orders began to come at a rapid pace. Everyone had a responsibility and settled into his job. This continued for seven long hours.

Bruce and his colleagues relieved each other in the ASDIC room as they tried to locate the submarine. As he said, the noise could drive a person "crazy". The closer the sounds came together, the closer the frigate was to the submarine.

Kapitanleutnant Heinz Rahe ordered the submarine to submerge further after the ship's radar had indicated that *Waskesiu* was nearby. The first depth charge had missed his ship. However, the second one was close enough to rock the submarine.

At 3:27 AM, contact was made again, with the submarine being about 1,500 yards (1.4 km) away and about 300 feet (90 m) deep. Lt.-Cdr. Fraser ordered a ten-charge attack. Contact was lost for about a half-hour. Then *Waskesiu* renewed its attack.

By now, Commander John Birch, who was aboard *Nene*, was aware of the presence of U-257. He ordered Fraser to withhold further attack until *Nene* had made contact with the submarine.

At 4:10 AM, *Waskesiu* made contact again. The submarine was running deep. Soon *Nene*, too, had made contact. Regrettably, the staff officer aboard *Nene* determined that what had been detected was not a submarine. Therefore, Commander Birch called off the hunt and ordered Waskesiu to return to the convoy.

Fraser was not ready to submit to failure. Therefore, he sought permission to continue for one more attack and was granted it. He sensed that his ASDIC crew should be trusted. Submarine contact was held until *Waskesiu* was about 350 yards (320 m) away. Then, the commander ordered a final ten-charge pattern. According to the ship's log, a total of 31 depth charges were dropped.

By this time, the submarine had been severely shaken and the main motors had been damaged. There were leaks in the control room and the engine room. Much water entered the submarine and its rudders were blocked. Knowing that his boat was helpless, the commander ordered his boat to the surface where *Waskesiu's* surface radar made contact with it at 5:50.

Then, U-257 was visually spotted. Lt.-Cdr. Fraser, who was on the bridge, saw her surfacing rapidly about 1,800 yards (1.6 km) ahead of his ship. He ordered his crew to fire star shells and to train the searchlights on it. Then he informed *Nene* of the submarine's presence.

With the submarine closer, the frigate's lights now illuminated the vessel. Her four-inch *(10-cm)* guns made four direct hits on the conning tower. The Oerlikon guns also hit the conning tower. With all this action going on around them, the order for the Germans to abandon their ship was given. The preparation for the exodus followed in orderly fashion.

Fred Rennie, who had been idly passing away his time, now realized that this was real action and swiftly bolted for the deck. To Clifford Adams, the action period seemed long, but otherwise routine. Then, when the sub surfaced and Thomas Stephenson was shooting at the Germans as they exited the tower, he, too, knew that this was not gunnery practice.

U-257 slowly crossed the frigate's bow to her port side. The frigate tried to ram the submarine. With the

enemy only 100 yards (90 m) away, Lt.-Cdr. Fraser could
not alter course in time to do so, as it was too close for
making the turn necessary to accomplish it.

However, he could hammer her with the #2
Oerlikon, which was manned by William Knox. It, too,
struck the conning tower. The Germans could not reach
their guns to answer back. As the Germans were coming
out the conning tower, the gunshots knocked about four
of them into the water.

Waskesiu's #1 Oerlikon did not waste a cartridge.
Her commanding officer stated that it was wonderful
gunnery. Stephenson downplayed his marksmanship by
saying that he could not miss at that range. The
submarine was a sitting duck.

During the action, the starboard searchlight failed. While Gerry Leahy and Gord Taylor were repairing it, ricochet bullets from another ship passed over their heads. They ducked down behind the canvas dodger. When it was over, everyone had a great laugh, thinking what protection they would have from a piece of canvas.

Water was entering the submarine, and the rudders were blocked. Despite all the noise of the impacting ammunition, the sailors did not panic. When the submarine began to sink, the Germans abandoned the ship.

The instant Art Wall, who was on #2 gun aft, pulled the trigger on the last shell fired, he knew the battle was over. The searchlight on the bridge illuminated the conning tower of U-257. A figure, assumed to be her commanding officer, became the cross in the crosswire of his gunsight. He was waving his arms apparently trying to signal their surrender. The gesture was foregone.

Fifteen minutes after surfacing, still under withering fire, U-257 had had enough. The sub's bow sank down, her stern reared up to nearly vertical, and she slipped under the roiling black waters.

The crew was elated that the battle had been completed in victory. There was a sense that this was revenge for the loss of *Tweed*. Now, they could return to convoy duty and some much-needed rest.

According to a news story in an English paper, it was the prayer of the men on HMCS *Waskesiu* that one day, before the war was over, they should sink a Nazi U-boat. Just a few weeks later, Waskesiu came upon U-257 and their prayer was answered.

According to Naval Intelligence Agency, British Admiralty, in June 1944, the official coordinates of the location of the sinking were 47°19'N., 26°00'W.

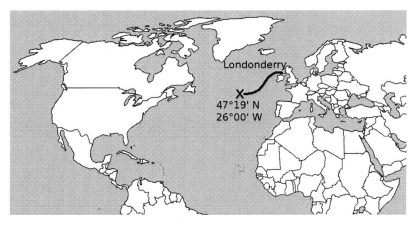

HMCS *Waskesiu* was the first Canadian frigate to sink a German submarine.

5

Rescuing the Germans

As the U-boat was sinking, her crewmen tumbled into the sea and life-jacket whistles shrilled. Lights from *Nene* indicated that there were German sailors in the water. From the water there was the call, "Hello, Kamerad! Hello, Kamerad!"

Whalers from *Waskesiu* and *Nene* were lowered into the heavy swells, and the Canadian and British ships began to pick up the survivors. However, the sea was too rough for *Waskesiu's* whalers. When two oars broke in the waves, the rescue attempt had to be concluded.

Waldemar Nickel, an officer on the U-257, had been in the water for forty-five minutes before being picked up by *Nene*. By 8:52 AM, that ship was able to pick up fifteen survivors while *Waskesiu* picked up only four.

Among the rescued were five chief and petty officers and a seaman who had been a survivor of a U-boat tanker supply ship. George Devonshire presumed that the survivors were the ones who had stayed below until after *Waskesiu* had checked fire and were lucky enough to leave the submarine before she sank.

Survivors of the sub later stated that *Kapitanleutnant* Franz Rahe, the U-boat's commanding officer, decided to go down with his boat, throwing his life jacket and his one-man dinghy to men in the water.

The Germans were given warm, dry clothes and hot coffee when they boarded. The naval action had now passed and the rescued were treated with respect and even friendship. The attitude had changed toward the enemy after the submarine had been sunk and the German sailors were struggling in the water. There is an unwritten law that sailors help other sailors in peril—friend or enemy.

Because of the rough sea and the darkness of the night, the ships had to leave the area and rejoin the convoy. The crews could hear stranded Germans still in the water, but were unable to help them.

After taking care of the rescued sailors, the crews became friendly with them. Some of the Germans had envisioned Canadians as being either cowboys or Indians. Some told of the destruction that the German Luftwaffe had inflicted upon Britain.

Over the next few days, the *Waskesiu* crew sized up their four prisoners. The sailors showed them the guns and charges that had destroyed their U-boat. They looked at the Canadians with silent contempt. The

Germans were later permitted
to join some of the sailors in
their mess deck to listen to the
radio. A couple of the ratings
collected their signatures.

They arrived in
Londonderry on February 28.
Army personnel were there to take the prisoners. The
Germans did not want to leave the Canadians, but said
goodbye to each other. The crew of *Waskesiu* had grown
to like them and believed the feelings of the Germans
reciprocated. However, the Canadians had not forgotten
Tweed, or that it might have been their ship.

According to ASDIC operator Andy Kaija, U-boats
were the greatest danger, and the enemy at the time
was to be destroyed. As for the U-boats' crew, their
hardships were great.

During the war, 661 Type VII C submarines were
built. As the war progressed, the Type VII C U-boats
received more and more anti-aircraft weapons. This
started with increasing the size of the conning
tower/sail to allow more mounting points and
culminated in eliminating the deck gun to increase the
AA capability. Starting in 1943, Type VII C U-boats were
fitted with the schnorkel, but by then the odds were
stacked against them.

U-257 participated in six patrols, but was not
responsible for any enemy ships being damaged or
sunk. The ship operated with the following Wolfpacks

during its career: Luchs, Falke, Landknecht, Seewolf, Adler, and Meise.

Nineteen crew members, including one officer, were taken as prisoners of war: Otto Cremer, Erwin Dielas, Franz Eberlein, Bernard Jungnitsch, Theo Kattelmann, Herbert Krug, Helmut Lenk, Egon Nehrkorn, Waldemar Nickel, Klaus Palm, Rudi Plate, Erich Reeger, Wilhelm Riewe, Herbert Schroder, Rolf Schroder, Helmut Schubert, Willi Siekmann, Fritz Sommer, Heinz Strempel.

Thirty seamen, including the commanding officer, died in the sinking of the submarine: Karl Arhelger, Heinrich Banck, Gerhard Buttner, Heinrich Butenschön, Friedrich Dalhoff, Josef Fischer, Hermann Fleck, Erwin Grys, Johannes Hocker, Hans Hohne, Reimer Hohne, Karl Holztrattner, Karl-Heinz Hufnagel, Paul Klemke, Rudolf Kloster, Karl Koch, Wolfgang Koditz, Werner Kunze, Karl Liedtke, Helmut Menzel, Heinz Rahe, Johannes Rauh, Gerhard Ringelsiep, Georg Saffer, Heinz Singer, Kurt Suchland, Franz Teigeler, Karl Wenzel, Heinz Werner, Karl Wichmann.

Specifications for U-257

Type: U-boat, VII C

Ordered: 23 DEC 1939

Laid down: 22 FEB 1941

Launched: 19 NOV 1941

Commissioned: 14 JAN 1942

Sunk: 24 FEB 1944

Displacement: 864.69 tonnes

Length: 67.10 metres (220 ft 2 in)

Width: 6.18 metres (20 ft 3 in)

Height: 9.60 metres (31 ft 6 in)

Depth: 4.74 metres (15 ft 7 in)

Crew: 44 men

Speed: 17.60 knots (20 mph, 33 km/h), 7.60 knots (9 mph, 14 km/h) submerged

Maximum Depth: 220 metres (722 ft)

Operating Radius: 8,500 km (5,300 mi) at 10 knots, 80 km (50 mi) at 4 knots submerged

Power Source: 2 MAN/GW diesel engines, 3,200 hp., 750 hp. submerged

Armament: 5 x 53.3-cm (4 bow, 1 stern) torpedo tubes with 14 torpedoes , 26 TMA mines , 1 x 8.8-cm (3½-in) L/45 gun on the deck , 1 x 2-cm (¾-in) and 1-3.7 cm (1½-in) anti-aircraft guns

6

Congratulations

Following are some of the communiques that the crew of *Waskesiu* received following the sinking of U-257.

> Enemy has been trying for more than three days to follow up success and have been using over a dozen U-boats. That he has entirely failed is due to your efforts and he has not escaped without damage. I congratulate you all, especially the carriers who have flown practically non-stop night and day.
> —General from Command Station #1

> Warmest congratulations and continued good hunting.
> —Flag Officer Newfoundland

> A grand effort and all alone you did it. My warmest congratulations to all on board for your fine achievement.
> —HMS *Nene*

Heartfelt congratulations on your well-deserved success.
—HMCS *Kootenay*

Congratulations on your success last night.
—HMCS *Gatineau*

Nice work. Congratulations!
—HMCS *Dunver*

Nice pitching mister. Congratulations.
—HMCS *Rosthern*

Your kid sister is very proud of you.
—HMCS *St. Catherines*

Well done Waskesiu. Welcome home.
—Commander-in-Chief, Northern Atlantic

6. Congratulations

Your 240618. Warmest congratulations.
—Commander-in-Chief, Western Atlantic

Well done. What is the story? How many
survivors?
—Staff Officer, Command #5

Jolly well done. Have you any 'non-sub'
survivors?
—Staff Officer, Escort Group #3

A Royal Canadian Navy official press release dated
Tuesday, April 4, 1944 reads as follows:

A United Kingdom Port—When the frigate
HMCS *Waskesiu* accounted for her U-boat, she
picked up four prisoners. The senior ship of
her support group, HMS *Nene*, picked up fifteen
including one officer.

When *Waskesiu* forced the U-boat to
surface, she poured such a withering fire into it
from her Oerlikons that the submarine's crew
had no chance to escape. Officers of *Waskesiu*
and *Nene* who were in a position to see the
whole action figure that those Germans who
were successful in escaping from the doomed
Nazi craft must have leaped overboard the
minute it surfaced. The rest went down with
their craft or were swept overboard by the hail
of gunfire from *Waskesiu*.

In the heat of the action, feeling in
Waskesiu, who engaged the U-boat and finally
sank her, ran high. Germans forced to take to

the water could be heard crying, "Hello, Kamerad; Hello, Kamerad!" in the darkness.

When the action was over, *Waskesiu* stopped long enough to pick up four survivors. One of the whalers was lowered in an effort to rescue other Germans, but because of a rising sea and a strong drift, the attempt had to be abandoned. Whalers from *Nene* picked up fourteen ratings and one officer.

When the German prisoners were taken on board Canadian and British ships, they cringed like men who expected blows. The most amazing thing to the officers of the two ships was the attitude of their own crews.

"The prisoners were no sooner on board than my men were brushing the wet hair out of their eyes, helping them off with their wet clothes, and wrapping them in blankets," said one Canadian officer. "After that the crew became quite friendly with the Germans and we were astonished one night to have one of the men make an appeal to have the prisoners allowed to go down on the mess deck and listen to the radio."

All the Germans were young. The average age was 22 and the oldest of the whole group was 26. Of them all, only one was a volunteer; all the rest were conscripts. All had the impression that Canadians were either cowboys or Indians.

When the Germans were put ashore, bound for an internment camp, their sodden, oil-soaked clothing had been replaced with new

warm woolens from extra supplies in the
lockers aboard *Waskesiu*. Offered their old
clothing, they declined with polite but firm
"Nein."

As the prisoners were taken down the
gangway at a British port, a Canadian seaman
leaned over the rail of his sleek frigate and
yelled: "Let this be a lesson to you, Jerry. You
better keep away from the water."

On April 4, Prime Minister Mackenzie King, who
represented the Prince Albert constituency, sent a
telegram to the mayor of Prince Albert, Saskatchewan. It
read as follows:

The Department of Naval Services is
announcing tonight that the frigate HMCS
Waskesiu, while engaged recently on escort
duty in the North Atlantic, after carrying out a
series of attacks with depth charges, destroyed
a U-boat which was attempting to attack a
valuable convoy. Survivors of the enemy ship
were subsequently made prisoners of war.

I am delighted to have the opportunity to
convey to you and through you to the citizens
of Prince Albert and to others who have such a
deep interest in the welfare of HMCS *Waskesiu*
and her crew, the news of this brilliant exploit
of the first frigate ever to be built in a Canadian
shipyard, and the first Canadian frigate to sink
a German submarine.

For the sinking of U-257, the Distinguished Service Cross was awarded to Lt.-Cdr. James P. Fraser and to Lt. John H. Lincoln, RCNVR.

The Distinguished Service Medal was awarded to AB Thomas Stephenson, AB John H. Rickard, and AB B. M. Stoner.

Those who received Mentioned in Despatches were Lt. James Farmer, engine-room artificer (third class); J. G. O'Brien; Petty Officer M. G. T. Fortune; and Acting Petty Officer A. F. McGee. In each case, the citation read: "For good service in the destruction of an enemy submarine."

Although every man had a part in the sinking, only a few received special commendation. The others may have been disappointed not to have been included.

7

Murmansk Run

On April 18, 1943, *Waskesiu* arrived at Scapa Flow, a large British naval base north of Scotland. The crew was issued parkas and large fur-lined sea boots. What was the purpose of the new gear? Rumours of an impending trip to Murmansk, Russia, passed through the ship.

Waskesiu joined a large escort which included two aircraft carriers, HMS *Fencer* and HMS *Activity*, numerous Royal Navy destroyers, a cruiser, USS *Milwaukee*, merchant ships, and Canadian frigates. The ships crossed the Arctic Circle on the 21st of that month on their way to Kola Inlet, Russia.

As soon as the convoy was under way, *Waskesiu*'s commanding officer informed the crew that they were on their way to Russia—which they had suspected. He warned his men to avoid Russian women if they did not want to be shot. All were instructed to behave themselves as this was among the first Canadian Navy ships to arrive in Russia.

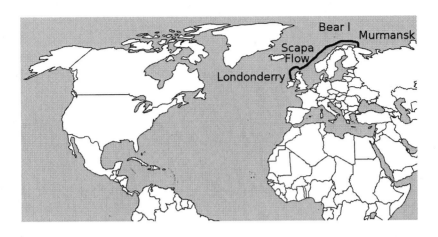

The real concern now was the water temperature. The sailors were told that they would last no longer than twenty minutes in the water.

All along the Norwegian coast huge floating mines were spotted. They were approximately 10 feet (3 m) long. Because of the long daylight hours, the crews could spot them quite easily. Nevertheless, they were a menace.

On April 22, one of the escort carrier aircraft sustained landing gear damage while attempting to land. The Swordfish ditched into the sea. A boat from *Waskesiu* was dispatched to pick up the two airmen—a successful mission.

On April 23, the convoy was about 12 miles (19 km) from Murmansk, and about 30 miles (48 km) from the Finnish front. The crew on *Waskesiu* could hear the big barrage guns and see Russian aircraft in the sky.

The ship tied up at Vaenga (Severomorsk), on Kola Inlet. After a harsh and dangerous passage, these sailors did not encounter tropical paradise. It was not

like Bermuda. The coastline was rocky and snowbound and the landscape was dotted with ruins and fallen planes.

Bud Lear reported that the Canadians stayed mainly near the jetty. It was such a bleak place. The people did treat them well. Children there wanted to trade with them for chocolate and gum.

Bruce Menzies stated that they always had to be on guard as they felt that could not trust them. Eventually, there was some trading of clothing for what turned out to be almost worthless paper money. The Russian women could barter better than the Canadian sailors and seldom lost in a deal. Then, there was the man who was willing to barter his wife for a few sweaters—but, no deal.

The sailors witnessed refugees from the nearby fighting wandering through the settlement. Uniformed women were building roads and digging ditches, while soldiers warily eyed the foreigners. Everyone seemed to be of equal status, working and living in much the same way.

The next day, some of the crew visited the town. The people lived in large structures that seemed like barns to the Canadians. They also saw a store where the residents dealt, and a post office.

When a couple of sailors disobeyed orders and tried to chat with some girls, they experienced Tommy-gun fire near them. They did not need any further persuasion. There was a report that, if a Russian girl were caught with a foreign serviceman, she would be sent to the front lines to fight. Most of the girls, as a result, would not look at the Canadians.

During their stay, one crew member became ill and was sent to the local hospital. Later, he was flown to Moscow and, eventually, back to England.

On that night, crews from some of the ships attended a Russian movie. It was all Soviet propaganda —very bad quality of film. Gordon Arnold reported that the sailors could not laugh because they feared that the Russians would misunderstand.

On April 25, some of the crew went sledding on a homemade sled. They found a huge hill where they enjoyed using their craft. Soon, they discovered that their hill was actually a factory. What a surprise that was!

On April 27, ten sailors from the cruiser USS *Milwaukee*, which had been transferred to the Soviets, came aboard *Waskesiu*. In all, 1,336 Americans were distributed in the convoy for the return trip.

George Devonshire remembered that the Americans were pleasantly surprised on learning that they would receive the traditional tot of rum with the rest of the crew. (US naval ships were dry.) When "up spirits" was piped, the Americans always seemed to be the first in line with their mugs.

About 1,430 Russian sailors boarded the merchant ships to be crew on ships which were in Great Britain waiting to be transferred to the Russians.

On April 28, convoy RA-59 sailed for Great Britain. The crew aboard *Waskesiu* watched—with a sense of relief—Vaenga recede in the distance. This was no place for them. It turned out to be the last trip for the summer, partly because of icebergs, but more because of the upcoming invasion of Europe.

The following day, U-boat reports began to be received. *Waskesiu* and her sister escorts conducted anti-submarine sweeps ahead of the convoy. It was bitterly cold and dark. Much action took place—day and night. There were dive bombers during the day and submarines at night. It was a nightmare, but *Waskesiu* survived.

On April 30, on numerous ships throughout the convoy, there were reports of periscope sightings. They were attacked by submarines, which had penetrated the outer screen. However, they met their match by the more numerous Royal Navy destroyers closer to the convoy. *Waskesiu* and the outer escorts closed in on the besieged convoy, dropping charges on submarine contacts.

Enemy aircraft appeared overhead, spotting the convoy for the massing U-boats. In an engagement, a German plane and a British Swordfish were shot down.

Following an unsuccessful sweep, *Waskesiu* and HMCS *Grou* returned to their stations. *Waskesiu* had just deployed its cat gear when the trail of a torpedo crossed *Grou's* bow. Suddenly, a young nervous sailor yelled, "Torpedo!" For some reason, his call was ignored. Even the captain did not take the call seriously.

Bear Island (Bjørnøya) is about 300 kilometres (186 mi) north of Norway. It belonged to Germany during the war, so they had submarine nests there. When *Waskesiu* departed the Murmansk area for the North Sea to the west, the crew knew that they had to pass Bear Island. Whether going south of it or north of it, they had to confront it. The ultimate decision was that they took the south passage for expediency, regardless of more danger because of possible sea and air attack from Norway as well.

According to Art Wall, when a torpedo hit was imminent, everyone was supposed to sit loosely on the deck. However, in this instance, the whole gun crew lined up on the starboard side to watch an acoustic fish pass beside their ship.

There was a terrific explosion as the torpedo hit their cat gear. A column of water shot straight upward astern of the ship. That was too close. The crew on *Grou* sent a message asking if they were hit, to which *Waskesiu* responded in the negative.

The cat gear is clanking metal bars at the stern of the ship to attract torpedoes away from the ship itself. The crew was a bit tired of putting out the cat gear and bringing it in again. After that, they were more cautious. Gordon Arnold observed that the Americans were very frightened on witnessing this action.

The actual action seemed to last about ten minutes to Cliff Adams. It was ten minutes of one explosion after another! The water and the air immediately above it were white from the explosions.

At one point, when the signal came to drop a depth charge pattern, Cliff released his three depth charges from the rail, but the first explosion seemed to be too soon because he could judge from the depth setting when his first depth charge should explode. In those split seconds, the first explosion must have been that of a German torpedo. It was rumoured that sixteen submarines were under the convoy as they sailed through.

Cliff further reported that submarine contacts continued over the following days, but the action was not as intense as on April 30. By May 3, the submarines were unable to reach the convoy.

There was a dogfight above the convoy on May 4, but it was out of sight for the *Waskesiu* crew. The convoy split up on May 5, with *Waskesiu* putting into Londonderry the next day.

The escort vessels of Convoy RA-59 received the following signal upon their safe arrival. "Enemy has been trying for more than three days to follow up success and has been using over a dozen U-boats. That he failed entirely is due to your efforts and he has not escaped without damage."

It had been a most difficult operation for the convoy. The sailors were very happy and relieved to be back in friendly waters. This was a very dangerous route by which the British freighters carried supplies to Russia.

The warships that were escorts for the convoy of about seventy-five freighters were as follows: from the Royal Navy, cruiser *Diadem*; escort carrier *Fencer*; aircraft carrier *Activity*; destroyers *Boadicea*, *Ulysses*, *Verulam*, *Virago*, *Walker*, *Whitehall*, *Marne*, *Matchless*, *Meteor*, *Milne*, *Musketeer*, *Beagle*, *Inconstant*, *Keppel*, *Westcott*, *Wrestle*; corvette *Lotus*; and from the Royal

Canadian Navy, frigates *Cape Breton, Grou, Outremont,* and *Waskesiu.*

The convoy was under constant attack from the Germans. During the night, U-boats would surface and shoot at the freighters. The warships could not use depth charges for fear of damaging their own ships. However, the defenders fought with the submarines the best that they could. During the day, they would be attacked by German dive bombers.

In addition, the sailors had to chip ice off the ship to prevent it from becoming top-heavy. If the boat were sunk, the freezing water would surely kill the sailors within five minutes.

In the run-on in which *Waskesiu* participated, no Allied warships were lost, but a few freighters were. Allied losses in the Arctic eventually exceeded those in the North Atlantic sea lanes. Before the war ended, the Arctic route had accounted for nearly 37% of all Allied surface ships sunk in all theatres of the war.

8

Near Disaster

On March 6, 1944, after being restocked at Londonderry, *Waskesiu* left for Moville, a town close to the northern tip of Ireland and about 30 km (19 mi) north of Londonderry.

On March 9, she left Moville with convoy EG6. The convoy also included the following ships: frigates HMCS *Outremont* and HMS *Nene*, corvettes HMCS *Edmunston* and HMCS *Prescott*, destroyer HMCS *Qu'Appelle*, and escort carrier HMS *Vindex*. Included was the sub-hunting group, EG2: HMS sloops *Starling*, *Magpie*, *Whimbrel*, *Wildgoose*, and *Wren*.

On March 11, she oiled up from a tanker. A U-boat was briefly sighted on the surface. No action followed as the U-boat escaped.

On March 16, while *Waskesiu* was refueling from the British escort aircraft carrier *Vindex*, an ASDIC contact was made. The pipeline was quickly cast off from the frigate. Moments later, a torpedo passed down the side of the carrier. The men on both ships wondered what would have happened if the torpedo had hit during the refueling process.

During the nine days that HMS *Vindex* was in the convoy, she lost three Swordfish, naval strike attack airplanes. These biplanes had a range of 770 miles (1,240 km) and could carry a torpedo, a mine, or eight 110-pound (50-kg) bombs. However, it was of little value against German fighters.

On March 24, a Swordfish crashed and burst into flames on the flight deck of *Vindex*. The fire crew was unable to extinguish the flames before it reached a depth charge. The crew of *Waskesiu* could see the flash and the fire. A whaler from the frigate picked up two airmen from the water and returned them to the carrier.

Waskesiu spent the following days patrolling off Northern Ireland, returning to Londonderry on the first of April.

9

On Patrol in the Channel

Something was about to happen. Was it the long-awaited invasion of France? On May 17, the escort group left Londonderry for Moville. The following days were occupied in work-up exercises with the aircraft carriers. On May 27, *Waskesiu* oiled up and set out toward England. That day, she dropped anchor at Moelfre Bay, on Anglesey Island, off the north coast of Wales.

On May 30, Commander Birch went to HMS *Liverpool*, a light cruiser, for a conference. In the succeeding days, as more Allied warships steamed into port, anxious seamen waited for word of the impending invasion.

On June 2, three aircraft carriers—HMS *Tracker*, HMS *Pursuer*, and HMS *Emperor*—moved into Moelfre. This heightened expectation for the invasion. There was no shore leave now, only mounting expectation. The crews of EG6 were put under two hours notice for steam. About forty ships—destroyer escorts, sloops, frigates, and carriers—now crowded the bay.

The crew had waited for a month for word on D-Day. They always had full steam up and had been sitting for two weeks in a bay, along with fifteen other warships.

Then, on the night of June 5, 1944, the captain was called for a meeting aboard HMS *Liverpool* with all the other captains. He returned with orders in a large brown envelope which was not to be opened until the ship had set sail. *Waskesiu* moved out at 4:00 AM.

The *Waskesiu*'s assignment, he told them, was to keep enemy submarines from entering the channel between Land's End, England, and Brest, France. The captain cheerfully said that they would all see their native land if every man did his job well.

Thus, it was going ten miles (16 km) one way and ten miles back for as long as it took for the landing in France to be completed. They were to protect the barges and troop ships crossing the channel. With other ships involved, both ends of the channel were blocked.

As they weighed anchor, all were mustered on the upper deck for the official message. Over the loud speaker, they heard, "This is Dwight Eisenhower, your Allied commander. We are on the eve of the invasion of the continent. Do your best and God bless."

When the invasion began, the sky was lit up as if it were the Fourth of July as the shells exploded. Two Allied warships were hit and sank in the English Channel. Being on the edge of the action, *Waskesiu* was less of a target for the shells.

It took two or three days for all the troops to cross. The Germans had a plan to invade England, but postponed the actual invasion until it was too late. Everyone had been waiting for about a year before the Allied invasion took place.

As *Waskesiu* performed her patrols, the crew saw thousands of bodies in the water. They were being carried by wave action, tide action, and the swells from the ships. The water was very choppy. They would pick up bodies as best they could, and then give them a proper sea burial. Fish had a tendency of eating the uniforms of the deceased airmen and soldiers.

Operation CA established the outer defence screen for the Allied Armada. About forty ships, assembled into six groups, patrolled the key western gateway to the channel, through which, it was thought, the marauding U-boats would pour from their Bay of Biscay ports.

Two of the CA groups were Canadian. Escort Group 9 consisted of the frigates *Matane, Swansea, Stormont, Port Colborne, Saint John,* and *Meon.* Escort Group 6 comprised *Waskesiu, Outremont, Cape Breton, Teme,* and *Grou.*

Their zone of operation was a vast swath of ocean, a 56,000-square-mile (145,000-km^2) rectangle extending from the channel mouth to a point off the Irish coast to another in the Bay of Biscay. As Allied armies stormed onto the beaches of Normandy, the ships of EG6 prowled the western approaches for U-boats. According to George Devonshire's account, the ships were not attacked by aircraft, as might be expected.

The various ships carried out many Hedgehog and depth-charge attacks on any kind of contact, whether it was classed as a sub or not. In the process, they killed thousands of fish rather than take a chance.

Reflecting on the relentless attacks, Art Wall wrote that he actually felt some sympathy for submariners and could not understand how so many escaped the pounding. Even his own ship was often badly shaken when there was an explosion—especially when set shallow. They had no idea how well built those submarines were.

Lt.-Cdr. Fraser believed that dozens of U-boats were destroyed. Most of them had probably died on the bottom where they were hit by depth-charges. However, there was no way of making sure that they had been destroyed.

A heavy swell was running on the dark night of June 10. The frigates HMCS *Teme*, HMCS *Cape Breton*, and HMCS *Waskesiu* had made several A/S sweeps with no success.

Teme was assigned to screen the aircraft carrier HMS *Tracker*. Moving his ship into position at 2:00 AM, Lt.-Cdr. Jeffery looked in horror as the carrier loomed out of the darkness on the port side, bearing directly on *Teme*.

The carrier struck *Teme* amidship, her bow axing a foot beyond the frigate's keel. Cut almost in half, the frigate's fore and aft bulkheads held fast under the savage blow. *Waskesiu* moved in to search for men in the water. None were spotted, but four men were lost. Taken into tow by HMCS *Outremont*, the sturdy warship was quickly repaired and put back to duty.

On June 13, bombers were sighted overhead. Without carrier protection, the anxious crew of *Waskesiu* strained to identify the aircraft. They were greatly relieved when they finally learned that they were Allied planes. The crew was most thankful that they were not enemy planes.

June 16 was a day of action stations. Though the results were once again negative, the crew brought up fish by the ton with depth-charges. After several more days of action stations, *Waskesiu* arrived in Moville.

Docking in Londonderry on June 22, *Waskesiu* was put into drydock for repair and refitting; and her crew was put ashore for rest and recreation. All were much needed.

On Monday morning, June 26, the crew reported back to *Waskesiu*—and the war. In their absence, the frigate's bottom had been checked and scraped, her stores freshly provisioned, and her armaments replenished.

When HMCS *New Waterford* arrived in Moville on the next day, hopes rose in the lower ranks of the *Waskesiu* that she might return to Canada for a refit. They were disappointed.

On June 28, *Waskesiu* sustained minor damage in a collision at the jetty, delaying leaving the port for another day. Escort Group 6 pulled out of Londonderry at 4:00 AM. On July 8, *Waskesiu* tied up at Portsmouth. Two of the watches were granted shore leave.

On July 10, *Waskesiu* was on patrol with HMCS *Cape Breton* and HMS *Rawley* when the British warship made sub contact. *Rawley* and *Waskesiu* dropped depth charge patterns. Before she could ascertain the results, *Waskesiu* was ordered to give assistance to a merchant ship about twenty miles (32 km) away.

On arriving at the scene she found that the merchantman was listing badly to the port side. It was thought that she may have struck a mine. While *Waskesiu* provided a screen, a corvette took her into tow.

The frigate was back in action on July 12. Rejoining her group on the next day, she passed the mail to adjoining ships.

Waskesiu was again in the English Channel on anti-submarine patrol along the Cherbourg Peninsula, within sight of the French coast. While the repeated negative results of depth charge attacks could be frustrating for her crew, they knew that, by harrying the U-boats, they were protecting the troops and equipment being transported across the channel.

On that day, the crew saw V-1 bombs, two of which were downed by ack-ack fire on the English coast. It was noted that 2,500 people had been killed by these "doodlebugs" by July 5.

Three days later, *Waskesiu* fired a Hedgehog pattern. This was of concern for the crew because of ammunition ships that had been sunk in the area. In her search for submarines, she also had to be concerned about the presence of mines in the water.

On July 28, *Waskesiu* dropped two five-charge patterns in response to a sub contact. The crew was at action stations for two hours. However, their only sighting was a merchant ship's empty lifeboat. Gunners sank that symbol of every sailor's potential fate.

July 29 was an eventful day. At 3:30 PM, shore batteries opened fire on incoming V-1s. Action stations sounded at 4:00 PM. The frigate dropped two five-charge patterns and fired the Hedgehog. More V-1s screeched through the air that afternoon. *Waskesiu*'s gunners were most anxious to fire on them, but they were unable to train their guns before they were out of range.

On July 31 at 1:00 PM, HMCS *New Waterford* relieved *Waskesiu*, which proceeded to Portsmouth for a brief layover, arriving two hours later. *Waskesiu* dropped a hook and took on fuel alongside a tanker.

The ratings were allowed leave for that day. On the next day, two watches were granted leave until 21:30 (9:30 PM). Throughout the day, troops moved out on barges. Aboard *Waskesiu*, the duty watch kept busy bringing on supplies.

Waskesiu weighed anchor at 8:50 AM on August 4, bound for A/S patrol in the channel. It was a hot, sunny day, and many of the crew on the upper deck removed their shirts. Hundreds of Allied bombers flew over the channel.

One day later, *Waskesiu* continued its patrol off the French coast near Cherbourg. Submarine contact was made at 1:30 PM. The frigate dropped two five-charge patterns—with no results.

Still patrolling the channel off Cherbourg on August 7, *Waskesiu* struck a buoy at 12:10 AM. In the darkness, many at first thought that a mine had been struck.

During the night, *Waskesiu* moved east to patrol the mouth of the Seine River. She was now patrolling with frigates *Grou* and *New Waterford* and the corvette *Drumheller*. *Waskesiu* was eight miles (13 km) from shore, and the war was close. The echoes of bombs and explosives hitting Le Havre could be clearly heard.

There was some excitement on the night of August 8 when, shortly before midnight, a bomb hit the water off the starboard bow. It also narrowly missed HMCS *New Waterford*.

One day later, *Waskesiu* moved to the Isle of Wight, where an aircraft had reported a surfaced U-boat. She patrolled the vicinity the following day, but made no contacts.

Relieved by HMCS *Annan* on August 11, *Waskesiu* pulled back into Portsmouth. At anchor the next day, some of the off-duty ratings passed the time swimming over the side.

Proceeding through the Strait of Dover on August 14, the frigate joined a convoy of three liberty ships. George Devonshire noted in his diary that this was at the height of the German V-1 buzz bomb offensive against London. The crew counted sixteen bombs flying over them in one hour. Leaving the convoy, *Waskesiu* steered for the harbour at Sheerness, at the mouth of the Thames River.

The flying bombs were again seen overhead in the early morning of August 15 as *Waskesiu* tied up to a buoy at Medway. The ratings had come to call it Hell's Corner because it was a dangerous spot for air raids and mines.

Waskesiu then made her way up the Thames River to London's East India docks. From August 17 to 24, the frigate had an overdue boiler cleaning. There was plenty of buzz bomb activity as they sat doing nothing in London. Nevertheless, the crew had an enjoyable time ashore—despite the bombs.

Waskesiu rejoined Escort Group 6 at Plymouth, participating in escort duties in the channel.

In summary, the D-Day fleet, under Admiral Sir Bertram Ramsay, included 7,016 vessels. Within that fleet were 110 ships of the Royal Canadian Navy, manned by 10,000 sailors.

10

Little Canada

Near the point where the Foyle River empties in Lough Foyle on the way to the Atlantic Ocean lies the city of Londonderry, or Derry as it is commonly called.

This port in Northern Ireland was like a home base to World War II Canadian warships involved in convoy escort and anti-submarine duties. The green grass along the banks, even in winter, caught the eye of many Canadian sailors as their ships entered the harbour.

Often there could be more than a dozen ships along the jetties either waiting orders or being stocked. The docks would be stacked with the needed supplies. Military and naval personnel with fixed bayonets stood guard.

Waskesiu would go out on patrol for about thirty days, then return to port for supplies. If it were more than thirty-five days, the food would be not much more than hardtack. After the ship had been restocked, she would go back into action for another thirty days.

As the ship entered the channel leading to Londonderry on one occasion, the crew lined up on deck as usual. On one shore was an old castle. Lined up on the green grass along the bank, with a deep blue sky was a group of Wrens waving undergarments in greeting. The sailors waved back and blew the ship's horn. The welcome lasted for about twenty minutes.

When the ship stopped, a depth charge was dropped, bringing up many fish. For supper that night and for two or three more days, the men had fish and chips to eat. Being from Montreal, Bruce Menzies was used to having fish every Friday.

The many Canadian sailors on shore leave always had something to do, whether it be going to pubs, restaurants, dance halls, or private homes. Some would spend a few days at a nearby resort for a little break. Others would go to Dublin.

Derry was always a welcome sight for the sailors. The residents welcomed these Canadians. They provided from their rations to make the best meals that they could for their visitors. The sailors appreciated their gesture very much. The Red Cross was instrumental in trying to provide for the needs of the sailors while they were in port.

German prisoners-of-war picked up at sea were brought to this port to be turned over to the British. Sailors of all ranks were noted for discussing their various activities on the ocean when there was a break from duty.

Although this was a British base, one would believe that it was Canadian because of number of Canadian sailors who could be seen in the port city during the war. Because St. John's was the other port for many ships on convoy duty, the term Newfie-Derry Run had become a byword.

However, it all came to an end on June 10, 1945. The return of Canadians to their homeland actually began a couple of weeks earlier.

One sailor reported that he and his buddies staged a dance and invited the citizens to attend as a farewell gesture of appreciation. The sailors carried with them their fond memories of this city and her people.

Farewell, Londonderry, you were a home away from home.

11

Final Days of War

HMCS *Waskesiu* eventually left EG6 to join C-3 in a westbound convoy, arriving in Halifax on September 17, 1944. George Devonshire stayed with the ship for a few weeks more as part of a skeleton crew, which sailed *Waskesiu* to Shelburne, Nova Scotia, for a much-needed refit.

While he was on leave in Montreal, Bud Lear sent a telegram to Captain Fraser. "Having a great time. Wish you were here. Request a further seven days leave."

The captain replied, "Glad you are having a good time. Save your money for war bonds. Extension not granted."

The majority of the original crew was transferred off the frigate here. Allan Tustian was one of the few to remain. Thus, he became used to another crew, mostly from HMCS *Magog*, which had been torpedoed in the St. Lawrence. Walter Ritchie was sad that he was one of those who left the ship and its wonderful crew after two years.

After her lengthy refit, *Waskesiu* returned to Londonderry, from where she continued A/S and escort duties. On December 14, 1944, Lt.-Cdr L.D. Quick became captain of *Waskesiu*. He remained in command until September 2, 1945.

In June 1945, after their European campaigns had been completed, *Waskesiu* returned to be refit at Shelburne for service in the Pacific Theatre. During the refitting, which lasted two or three months, the men had leave.

After reassembling in Shelburne, they proceeded to Halifax on *Waskesiu*. The ship was part of a convoy. On arrival, everyone saluted. There was a large welcoming crowd on shore. The men were given leave to go home. The warship was still undergoing tropicalization when the war ended.

Her crew suffered no casualties in a year of action. Surgeon-Lieutenant R. S. MacFarlane did not have even a cut finger to repair. He felt that he had a good sick bay on the ship, but no business for it.

The camaraderie in the original crew partly evolved from pride in their shared distinctions. HMCS *Waskesiu* was the first Canadian-built frigate and the first of its class to sink a U-boat. She was among the first RCN frigates to land in Russia, and she was in the thick of action in Operation Neptune, in support of the Normandy invasion.

With at least three near misses from torpedoes and one U-boat kill to her credit, Arthur Wall remarked, "I always felt *Waskesiu* was a lucky ship."

11. Final Days of War

Although it was largely unprepared for war in 1939, Canada's navy grew until it eventually provided 47% of all convoy escorts. Rear Admiral Murray, Commander-in-Chief North-West Atlantic, who directed convoy battles from Halifax, would become the only Canadian to hold an Allied theatre command during the war.

By 1945, the Royal Canadian Navy comprised 378 fighting ships and 95,000 uniformed men and women. It had suffered 2,210 fatalities, including six women, and a loss of 24 warships. It had destroyed or shared in the destruction of 33 U-boats and 42 enemy surface craft.

The navy escorted 25,343 merchant vessels across the Atlantic. These ships carried 181,643,180 tons of cargo to Europe—the equivalent of eleven lines of freight cars, each stretching from Vancouver to Halifax.

Between 1939 and 1945, over 1,700 Merchant Navy personnel lost their lives from enemy action. This figure includes Canadian seamen who were lost while serving aboard 278 Canadian and Allied ships. Most of the Merchant ships were sunk in the Battle of the Atlantic.

12

Crew of HMCS *Waskesiu*

Acomplete list of the crew is no longer available. Bruce Menzies advised that he had tried unsuccessfully to obtain one. However, he was able to locate many names after months of work.

Lt.-Cdr. Graeme Arbuckle, Navy Heritage Officer for the Directorate of History and Heritage, Ottawa, Ontario, sent us the following information. "Unfortunately, there is no way of knowing who was actually serving in the ship at any given time. Records of this sort were not kept; rather it was the individual members whose records show which ships they served in. Only possible way to do this would be to research the records at Library and Archives of Canada— something we do not do on behalf of others."

This is a partial list as garnered from newspaper articles, photos, and other records. Note that only last names are given. There are two reasons for this. (1) We have been able to obtain many, but not all, of the first names. (2) In the navy everyone was known by surname only and knew only a few close contacts by the first name also. Thus, this list follows the naval tradition.

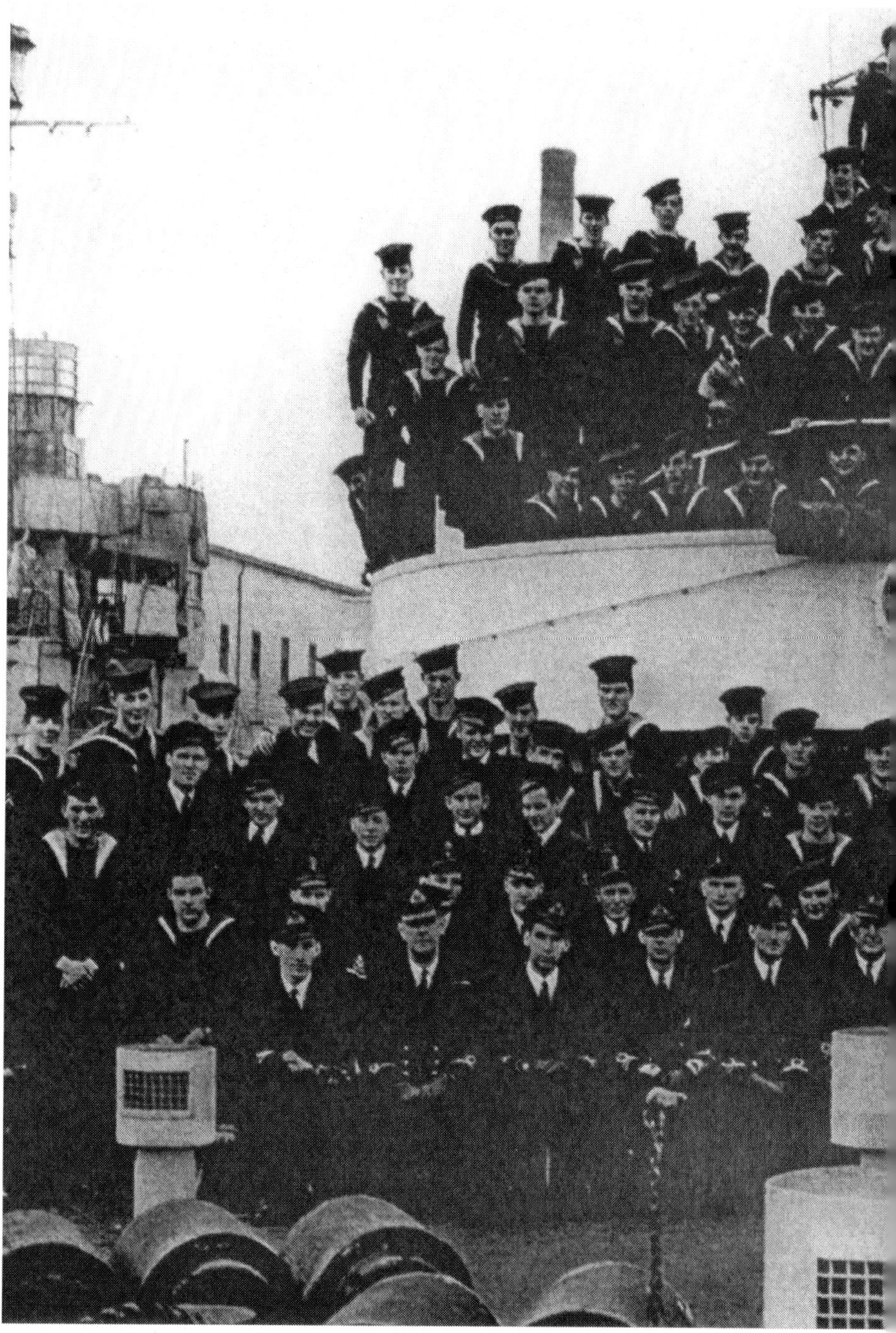

12. Crew of HMCS *Waskesiu*

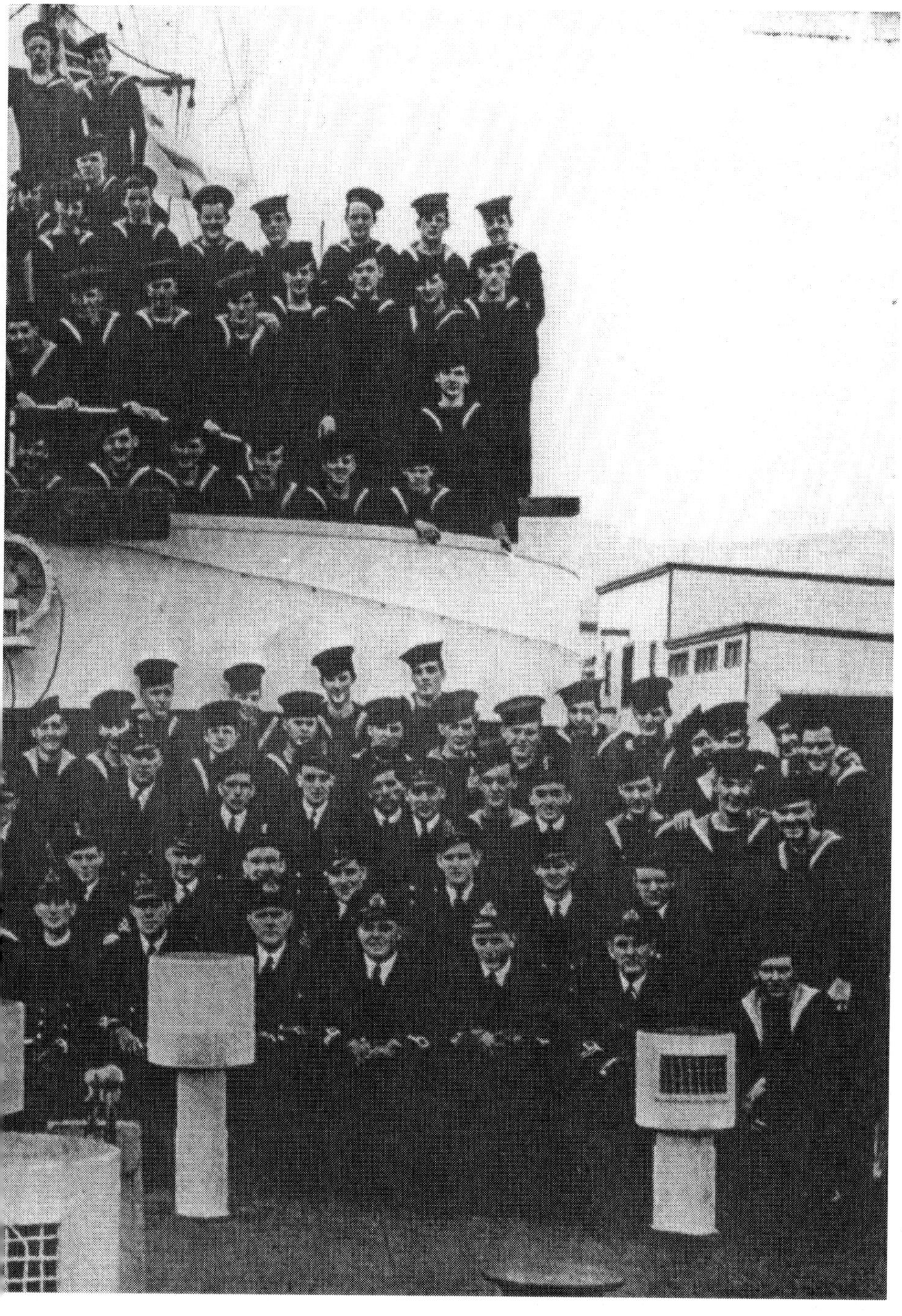

Commanding Officers:

Lt.-Cdr. Macdonald (16 JUN 1943—4 FEB 1944),

Lt.-Cdr. Fraser (5 FEB 1944—13 DEC 1944),

Acting Lt.-Cdr. Quick (14 DEC 1944—22 OCT 1945)

Other Officers:

Lt. Farmer, Lt. Holmes, Sub-Lt. Irvine, Lt. Lincoln, Surgeon-Lt. MacFarlane, Lt. McLeod, Lt. McPhee, Lt. Manson, Lt. Nares, Lt. Rennie, Lt. Williams, Padre *(surname unavailable)*

12. Crew of HMCS *Waskesiu*

Non-Commissioned Officers and Ratings:
Adams, Agnew, Arnold, Arsenault, Bachan, Bertand,
Bichard, Booth, Borne, Burns, Burton, Buse, Casey,
Chalmers, Cook, Courtney, Dawson, Dennan,
Devonshire, Dixon, Farley, Findlay, Fogg, Fortune, Frey,
Fontaine, Gibb, Grandy, Harasyn, Hartley, Hatch,
Hirtle, Jenkins, Johnstone, Joyal, Kaija, Knox, Law,
Leahy, Lear, MacGreoy, McGee, McGregor, Machalek,
Menzies, Makowelchuk, Miller, Muggah, Murray, Nauss,
Nott, O'Brien, O'Hearn, Parker, Paterson, Power, Reid,
Rickard, Ritchie, Robinson, Ross, Rudland, Rushton,
Sawchuk, Sheaves, Slaven, Stephenson, Stoner, Talwin,
Tanning, Taylor (G.), Taylor (W.), Testan, Turner,
Tustian, Vachon, Vanstone, Venner, Walker, Wall,
Watts, Webb, White, Willis, Worsencroft.

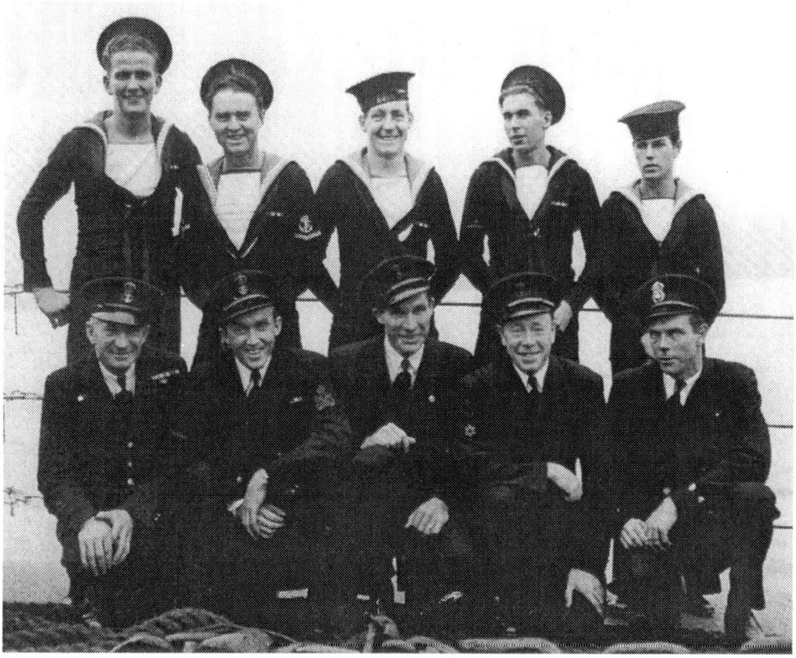

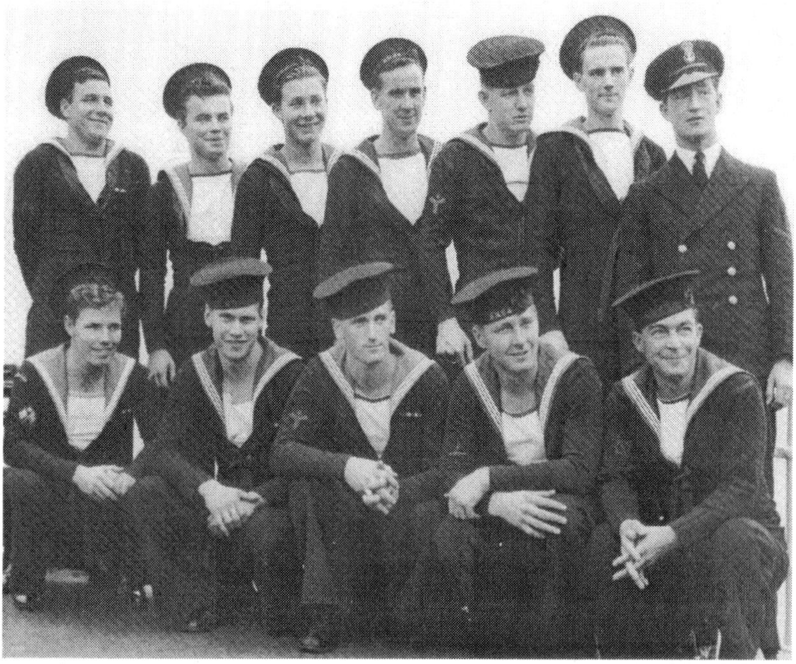

13

Cliff Adams

As far as he knew, none of his shipmates ever considered being tattooed—but there was one exception. That sailor, who was from Prince Edward Island, was a good-natured Able Seaman with good living habits.

To the amazement of all, when he returned from a shore leave, he sported a beautiful tattoo of Jesus Christ on the cross. When Cliff asked why he had it, he preferred not to comment. He probably suspected what the reaction might be. Thus, there were no more questions.

However, long after, in 1988, when on vacation in Prince Edward Island with his wife and his daughter, Cliff inquired for his former shipmate. Someone gave directions to a lobster shed in a small village. On arriving there, he learned that the person had died a year before. That was a disappointment.

However, the next morning in Charlottetown, he received a telephone call. It was his friend. What a marvelous turn of events this was! There had been confusion because of the number of people with the same last name living in that village.

His friend, who had been single when Cliff knew him, now had a wife and twelve married children—six sons and six daughters. It was with inward gratification that Cliff was able to witness the saga of a yearlong shipmate and see how well he had fared in his life.

However, there was one unanswered question. "How about that tattoo?" Now he was willing to confide.

His friend said that he was on watch alone when a huge wave swept him right into the sea and another huge wave swept him right back onto the ship's deck. That was why he obtained the tattoo the next time he went ashore.

Some would say that this happened by chance—if at all. Others would give a scientific explanation for the phenomenon. However, to this young sailor, it was much more than either.

He had a spiritual experience, and the tattoo was his way of giving thanks for his miraculous rescue. Cliff was satisfied that his question had been answered.

Cliff was born in New Westminster, British Columbia. He claims that his prior sea training was in the Academy of Hard Knocks. He had spent the summer of 1938 in commercial fishing.

He was in the navy from 1943 to 1945. He took his basic training at HMCS *Tecumseh* in Calgary; at HMCS *Naden* in Esquimalt; and at HMCS *Comox* in Comox, British Columbia.

He served aboard HMCS *Waskesiu* as a seaman torpedo man and later transferred to Supplies Branch at the land base HMCS *Avalon* in St. John's, Newfoundland. He was disappointed that he was not assigned to go to sea again.

After waiting in Halifax manning depot for a couple of weeks in 1943, he was excited to hear his name called for drafting to a ship. He boarded with his gear in the dark about 10:00 PM and found that another seaman torpedo man was boarding as well.

This sailor turned out to be George Devonshire. He was trained in Quebec City, whereas Cliff was trained in Victoria. The ship was HMCS *Waskesiu*, which was bound for St. John's.

Floundering in the darkness, he tried not to look too green, but certainly found it different to wend his way to duty watch from the mess deck to the quarterdeck at the stern.

There he became acquainted with Bill Hartley and Irving Agnew of the blue watch. Both had joined the Royal Canadian Navy as boy seamen. They were veterans at an early age. Now, it was their job to break in a greenhorn.

In charge of their mess deck was Leading Seaman John Rickard. They sat across from each other at breakfast. Cliff poured too much milk into his dish of porridge and, with the sway of the ship, the milk spilled over to the opposite side of the table. Welcome to the high seas, Clifford!

The food aboard *Waskesiu* was good, considering the difficulties created by sea conditions. On shore, it was satisfactory.

If *Waskesiu* were to dock long enough in Londonderry, the sailors occasionally stayed at a rehab camp at Port Rush. It is a summer resort town near Port Stewart. The camp was a good retreat. They could stay at Port Stewart—at their own expense—if they desired.

Cliff has experienced numerous bed and breakfasts during his life. However, the dinner and breakfast at that one in Port Stewart were the best. Vegetables were so well prepared. The hearty breakfast would satisfy the hunger of any British Columbia logger.

On one occasion, he went below deck to visit Johnny Douglas on his corvette, which was also in Londonderry harbour. They had been pals in elementary school in Burnaby, BC.

He was astounded by the cramped living quarters. Johnny explained how the sea would sometimes wash right down into the living quarters. Cliff felt sorry for him. He offered his friend a cigarette.

Johnny refused it, stating that he was staying in shape and away from any bad habits. It was his goal to be ready to play lacrosse again after the conclusion of the war. Eventually, he did play again—and well enough to be inducted into Canadian Lacrosse Hall of Fame.

He found his own living conditions at sea satisfactory. Although he made five crossings to Ireland in convoy duty, the return entrance to St. John's harbour was a joy to behold. The narrow entrance spelled security and the citizens were hospitable and considerate.

There were three men on the blue watch. At times, especially when weather was bad, one of them would be alone at the phone station and the other two would be inside and sheltered in the workshop. They rotated during the four-hour watch.

On such solitary occasions, Cliff would observe a corvette as it protected its allotted section of the convoy. The corvette crew numbered ninety, whereas the frigates carried one hundred fifty.

In the high sea, he would watch a corvette as it mounted the crest of a wave and observe it sink out of sight down into the trough. How was it possible that it would always reappear? But, it did. That was one way of passing time when on watch.

The crew played records of popular music on the ship's public address system. In port, they played the Mills Brothers' "Paper Doll". Some said that it was their theme song. While cleaning up the mess deck area prior to such inspections as Captain's White Glove routine, they listened to BBC radio broadcasts on the public address.

It was mentioned that Glen Miller and his orchestra were in London and were playing for the troops. Therefore, when Cliff was at the Maple Leaf Club, he asked the lady in charge of free tickets if she had a ticket for the Glen Miller band appearance. Her reply in heavy Cockney accent indicated that she had never heard of the American band leader. Being disappointed, he pursued it no farther.

When HMS *Tweed* was lost on January 7, 1944, Cliff arrived on deck just in time to see the ill-fated ship sinking upright into the sea. The German submarine U-305 had fired three torpedoes, one just missing *Waskesiu* and one hitting *Tweed.*

In the battle with the submarine U-257, he dropped depth charges and manned a sea boat in a rescue attempt.

An auxiliary aircraft carrier gave him a frightening experience. After closing off from a routine action station when no serious submarine contacts occurred, all naval vessels were ordered to return to their respective positions in the convoy.

It was daylight and about 6 or 7 PM. He described the criss-crossing of the ships like a city intersection where one car does not stop for a red light. He was at the extreme stern end of *Waskesiu.*

He saw the carrier bearing down on his position. Would there be a collision? He was in line for it if there were. What a sigh of relief he gave as it passed by! He wondered if any others aboard witnessed it as dramatically as he did. One goes on with what needs to be done regardless of distractions.

In Ireland, the sailors would often be granted leave when the ship was in port for a few days. On one leave, George Devonshire and Cliff went to London. With a name like Devonshire, he was bound to have relatives in England.

George had advised his aunt that the two friends intended to call on her. She lived in an attractive apartment which seemed to be quite large. Even in wartime, she had a butler who looked after the serving of dinner. It was a wonderful change from navy food and dinner routine.

On another leave, he and George visited his cousin. It was at the time when buzz bombs were regularly dispatched from Germany. The cousin had an Anderson air raid shelter. It was a metal frame and fit under a double-size bed. The three of them dived into the shelter and waited. When the bomb exploded nearby, his cousin remarked, "Beastly incredible, isn't it?" Happily, she survived the war.

On one more occasion, he visited George's aunt when his friend did not have leave. He had purchased gifts in Newfoundland for her, so Cliff did the honours.

The final visit to his aunt came when *Waskesiu* was at the East India docks in London. They went up the Thames for repairs, which took a week. When George could not reach his aunt by telephone, they went to her apartment building.

What a shocking sight met their eyes! It had been demolished. The only remnant was a rake hanging on a flat brick wall about three storeys up. George telephoned another cousin and happily found his aunt there. Presumably, she had gone to an air raid shelter during the raid.

Once while the ship was in for repairs, they were given leave and went to the Maple Leaf Club, in London, for accommodation. It was late in the afternoon.

As they walked up the staircase, they met several frightened uniformed women. They were Red Cross workers, who had arrived from Canada that day. When the buzz bomb warning wailed, they had no concept of what to do. The sailors did what they could to help them calm down—to the extent of escorting two of them to a popular Piccadilly Chinese restaurant for dinner.

One day, when he was on leave alone in London, he was riding a double-decker bus. A lady behind him touched him on the shoulder and asked, since he was from Canada, would he like to tour the British Houses of Parliament. The invitation was immediately accepted. She told him to meet her at a certain gate the next morning at a particular time.

When Cliff arrived, the guard asked for his name and if he were expecting to see a certain lady, and then ushered him in to meet the lady. She showed him where Charles I had been beheaded in 1649. Then, she escorted him through the House of Commons and the House of Lords (which was in session). Finally, she placed the seal of Britain into his hand.

This guide was secretary to the Chancellor of the Exchequer, thus the access to the Parliament Buildings —even in wartime.

Cliff received the following medals: North Atlantic Medal; French/German Star; 1939-1945 Star;

Volunteer 1939-1945; three Russian medals; memorial medals; British Arctic Star.

On his home-coming, he made up his mind to obtain more education. Thus, he directed his attention to the University of British Columbia.

Over the years, Veteran Affairs Canada has taken care of many veterans. He feels that they deserve recognition for their dedicated attention.

Cliff currently lives in Surrey, British Columbia.

14

Gordon Arnold

How very boring and cold it was, especially at night! He would climb up a rope ladder on the tallest mast of the ship and then work his way into his barren station. This was the crow's nest—the size of a barrel—where he would sit for four hours before having four hours off.

Comfort was not a consideration in the navy. It was his responsibility to report any obstacles on the sea and to keep alert for anything. What could he see at night—and stay awake?

Gordon was born in Ottawa, Ontario, on September 23, 1923. Before he entered the navy in December 1940, he was a member of Cameron Highlanders of Ottawa. While he was still in high school, he started as a carrier for the Montreal *Gazette*, picking up his newspapers at 5:00 AM, and worked up to be manager of the carriers in his region of Ottawa.

As he was very anxious to join the Royal Canadian Navy, he misconstrued his age. To accomplish this, he went to St. John's Anglican Church in Ottawa and asked for his birth certificate. Since he was working for the Montreal *Gazette* at the time, he went to the manager of the local office who used invisible ink in his copy work. Gordon obtained some and used it to alter his birth certificate so that he could enter the service underage.

He did not want anyone to know that he was too young because of the risk of being sent home. Therefore, he kept a very low profile and went about his duties quietly.

He took his basic training in Toronto and Halifax. He was an Ordinary Seaman and was responsible for various deck duties, but never that of swabbing decks. In addition to HMCS *Waskesiu*, he served at Halifax, Shelburne, HMCS *Naden* (Victoria), and on HMCS *Toronto*, HMCS *Reo II*, and HMCS *Copper Cliff*.

When he became a member of the crew of *Waskesiu*, food was rationed. It was his responsibility to follow a strict code as he passed out food supplies to the lower deck. There was usually sufficient food, but no luxuries on board ship. However, food for the sailors bore no similarities to that at home.

Drinking water was kept in a tank below deck. The sea temperature kept it cool. It could not be used for bathing—only for drinking. The tank would be refilled in Londonderry when supplies were obtained.

His living quarters were clean, but he missed not having a radio. He spent his free time reading fiction books of many authors as he was a member of a book club. One genre of book that did not interest him was romance.

Everyone had to keep his hammock and personal items tidy. There were small lockers—not metal ones—built along the lines of the ship. There was room for the uniform and underwear, but for not much more. Outdoor gear was hung in a wet room.

At the time of the battle with U-257, he was working with communication head phones in an area of the ship between #1 gun and the bridge. He communicated with the bridge—he thinks probably the gunnery officer. As he received coordinates, he passed them on to the gun layers.

He was young and not afraid of anything. He did not know what fear was. When the other fellows came off watch on the Murmansk Run, they went to the upper deck and crowded around the smoke stack. However, Gordon would strip off his clothes, mount his hammock, and go to sleep.

Just before D-Day, *Waskesiu* was moored at Moelfre Bay, North Wales. The crew was allowed to go ashore to the village of Belleck, but in civilian clothes to avoid drawing attention to them. Many of the sailors headed for the pubs. However, he wandered about the seaside as he was not one to go to pubs in those days.

Moelfre Bay was where a British submarine went down when on trials. From this place, *Waskesiu* headed for its position in the English Channel for the European invasion.

What impressed him the most on board *Waskesiu* was the church services on Sunday. First officer Lincoln obtained an organ, brought it aboard to the

quarterdeck, and would play it at services. There were two types of service aboard—a Catholic and a Protestant. The Catholics met below deck.

The poverty of the people in Londonderry made a big impression on Gordon. However, he found them very congenial. He considered the city a pleasant place, despite it being wartime. When his ship would go to St. John's, he would pick up some treats for friends in Londonderry for his next visit.

One time, he was invited to a home for dinner. Since there were no chicken eggs available, his hostess served him either a goose egg or a duck egg. It was so unappetizing! However, he suffered through eating the egg rather than embarrass the family.

The sailors showed their appreciation for the people of Londonderry just before leaving for the last time. They organized a big dance and invited the townspeople to it.

He was awarded the following medals: 1939-1945 Atlantic Star; 1939-1945 France and Germany Star; 1945-1985 Russian Anniversary; 1945-2005 Russian Anniversary; Royal Navy Arctic Star.

He described his homecoming as being very quiet. He had been away from his family for approximately five years. After the devastation that he witnessed in England and Murmansk, Russia, he was very grateful that he was able to return to his home town of Ottawa. Many people did not have a home in which to go in those countries.

After the war, he joined the public service as a clerk II. Eventually, he received an appointment as administrative ship's writer to the first Canadian Hydrographic Survey ship (converted former HMCS *Fort Frances*), and continued this career for twenty-nine years. During that time, he made two trips with CGS *Baffin* over the Arctic Circle in 1959.

Gordon currently lives in Nepean, Ontario.

15

George Devonshire

It was a terrible sight to behold! For the first time he was witnessing a ship sinking. This was his most lasting memory of his experiences in the navy.

Waskesiu was one of three ships doing patrol duty in the Bay of Biscay, off the French coast, where there were several enemy bases. The ships were sailing abreast, about a mile (1.6 km) apart.

One torpedo passed close by the bow of *Waskesiu* while another continued straight for HMS *Tweed*. It was a fatal blow, as the ship sank very quickly with a heavy loss of life. Every sailor knew that, in time of war, the potential of this fate lurked over him. As he watched *Tweed* sink, he sadly wondered why the Allies always seemed to lose a battle. Would they also lose the war?

George was born in Toronto on February 17, 1923. In his youth, he was a member of Toronto Sea Cadet *Temeraire* from 1938 to 1941. Before entering the Royal Canadian Navy for three years, he was in Canadian Merchant Navy for one year.

In April 1942, he joined the Canadian National Steamship Lines in Montreal. He served aboard the

Danish ship MV *Asbjørn* as a galley boy, working for ten hours a day and seven days a week.

Asbjørn was a general cargo ship. Because Denmark had been occupied by the Germans, the ship was under charter to the Canadian government to haul munitions and war materiel to the United Kingdom. He found out later that the total cargo on his first trip was 500 tons of TNT and 250 tons of picrate, another explosive.

The bombs had lifting rings in the noses and were without tailfins. They were hoisted four at a time from the dock and dropped through the hatches to four stevedores with hand carts and then wheeled into position and set down on end.

There was a gang of carpenters who laid plank floors between the many layers of bombs to pass between the rings, which projected above the floors. As soon as a floor was completed, a new level of bombs would be placed and the process was repeated.

He was happy when the cargo had been delivered. Welcome to the Merchant Navy!

On the way back to Canada, there was some excitement. About 10:00 PM on August 3, he was aroused and told to dress for lifeboats. As a young man, he was much amazed with the sight when he arrived on deck. He described it as like a really expensive May 24.

The convoy was under attack. Gunfire could be seen in the sky and heard on all sides. Although there was a call for "lifeboat ready", no one had to leave the ship. George was too excited to be frightened. Sleep for the rest of the night was impossible. His ship arrived safely at Quebec City on August 11.

He took his basic training for the Royal Canadian Navy in Quebec City, Cornwallis, and Halifax, after which he was in the Seaman Torpedo Branch, graduating at the top of his class. He served on HMCS *Waskesiu* for 420 days and also on numerous shore bases.

On board, he found his living quarters rather cramped. There would be more than thirty men sleeping in the mess deck at one time. It was an area of approximately thirty feet by thirty feet (9 x 9 m), with small racks on each side. The hammocks were lashed above the dining tables. Thus, the men ate where they slept. It could be hot or cold there, depending upon the weather. Therefore, on the Murmansk Run, it would be quite cold.

He stated that the food on *Waskesiu* was okay, but described that on the corvettes as "Yuck!" Food quality on board *Waskesiu* depended upon the weather.

If the weather was bad, it was very difficult to keep on the stove food that was being prepared, since more than one hundred men were being served each day. This created much pressure on the cooks. The men would have similar problems at their tables. However, it was better when the weather was calmer.

At first, his job was to set the hydrostatic pistols to explode the depth charges at various depths as ordered from the bridge. Ten depth charges would be fired in one attack—three each from the two stern rails and one each from the four mortars on the sides of the ship. After each firing, new depth charges had to be put into place for the next firing.

During the battle with U-257, he operated the Hedgehog. His highlight in this position was having a ringside seat during the battle with the U-boat.

The Hedgehog was made up of twenty-four contact bombs on spigots at the bow of the ship ahead of the guns. The ship would approach a target at slow speed. If the bombs did not hit the target, there was still a connection with it because of the slow movement of the ship. It could reconnect easily and, therefore, not have to search again.

The exploding depth charges created problems with sonar reception. It was difficult to regain contact quickly after ten charges had exploded as they would be going off in less than a minute.

There was another set of smaller ones having a sensitive fuse. There was one connection between the bombs so that they landed in a wide pattern and all would detonate.

There was never really a successful attack with the Hedgehog. The main reason was that the instruments were not up-to-date, thus making it difficult to ascertain when the actual firing would occur.

When *Waskesiu* was at Shelburne, Nova Scotia, for refitting after completing its tour of duty in European waters, George stayed on board as part of a skeleton crew. Then, after a 60-day leave, he returned to torpedo school in Halifax for more training. He also attended

112

seamanship school at the dockyard and passed his course for leading seaman.

While he was in class, VE-Day came. The school was closed and the gangway was declared open. As sailors poured into the city, liquor stores, bars, and restaurants were closed. The infamous riots followed. George felt that this was a shameful way to end a war.

George feels that it was a very exciting time when he was in the navy. He saw places in the world for the first time and would not likely see them again.

Probably the most notable place for him was Londonderry. The ship would enter the estuary from the Atlantic Ocean and go up the Foyle River for a short distance at a slow speed. He was fascinated in seeing green grass in winter—right up to the edge of the river. This was a most serene experience after the rigours of the North Atlantic.

Overall, George was away from home for five years, but had two visits during that time. For his service, he was awarded the Atlantic Star and two routine medals. After the war, he was a business executive.

In recent years, he carried on correspondence with a German survivor from U-257, Waldemar Nickel. George and his wife Phyllis hosted the gathering of the former sailors at Pinyer's Cove, Ontario, which Waldemar and his wife Carmen attended. There was so

much respect for each other and for the former enemy. For George it was a very remarkable experience in meeting after so many years.

George currently lives in Picton, Ontario.

16

Claude Joyal

He was AWOL when *Waskesiu* left Plymouth, England. He must be aboard his ship! Therefore, he managed to locate a hovercraft take him to it.

The captain was not sympathetic. The discipline he meted out to the late arrival was having him swab a deck, a common punishment.

He grabbed a mop and a bucket of water. Then, he began to carry out his sentence. It was not an easy undertaking trying to keep that bucket under control as the wave motion of the sea rocked the ship, causing the bucket of splashing water to be on the go—back and forth. He had swabbed the officers' deck as regular duty, but this was not regular duty.

Claude Edward was born in The Pas, Manitoba, on September 28, 1920. He served in the Royal Canadian Naval Voluntary Reserve from 1942 to 1945.

After taking his basic training at HMCS *Chippewa*, in Winnipeg, he served on HMCS *Waskesiu* from the time that it was commissioned until about two months prior to the war's end. He verified that all commanders were well-liked by the sailors.

Before he left Esquimalt for Halifax, he was aware of a riot in Vancouver which involved sailors. However, even though he was ashore, he did not take part in it.

He remembered stopping at several places en route to Halifax, especially Guantanamo Bay, the American base in Cuba, and in Bermuda.

He worked mainly on the afterdeck with depth charges, learning on the job. His job was to lay them on the racks.

He stated that meals were very good. However, there was an instance when the food supplies ran low because the ship was on escort duty for a period of thirty-one days and could not replenish the supplies.

The living quarters were where they ate, socialized, and slept. Hammocks had to be slung directly above the dining tables, then lashed, and stowed away after use, daily. He enjoyed sleeping in a hammock, being rocked to sleep by the motion of the ship and sleeping like a baby.

There was a laundry room where the men washed their clothes. This was accomplished by hand, without a machine. He used a brush to keep the lint off his bells. He was unaware of the use of adhesive tape used later to do this job.

He spent much time in writing letters when it was quiet on his off time. Like many of the men, he kept a diary of daily occurrences. He also used this time to perform his personal mending.

It was January 7, 1944, at approximately 4:12 PM while Claude was on deck working the Hedgehog at the bow of the ship, when a torpedo passed in front of him. That was too close. As he watched its movement, it struck HMS *Tweed*. Numerous explosions followed. Like other crew members, he noted that she went down in just a few minutes after a torpedo hit her.

At the time of the battle with U-257, Claude had just gone off duty from the previous shift. He was standing at mid-ship on the starboard side observing the action when the submarine was brought to the surface.

The Murmansk Run was an experience which he could not forget. What he remembers most about living conditions on this trip was the great amount of ice which collected on the ship. The men had heavy outer clothing on this trip. The head gear, which was not a parka, had eyelets for the use of buttons.

On one leave, he took a trip to London. From there, he took a train trip to visit Wales. On another leave, he took a train trip to Scotland.

At his homecoming, he had a reunion with his wife, parents, and friends. He had been away from home for two and one-half years, but he had a leave during the autumn of 1944 and returned to *Waskesiu* after the leave.

He was awarded the following: 1939-1945 Star, France and Germany Star with Atlantic Clasp, Canadian Volunteer Service Medal with Clasp, 1939-1945 War Medal, Commemorative Russian Medal.

After leaving the navy, he worked in a variety of jobs: labourer, bookkeeper, warehouseman, shipper, salesman, officer manager, and purchasing agent.

Claude currently lives in The Pas, Manitoba.

17

Walter (Bud) Lear

He was an eavesdropper at Harbour Grace, Newfoundland, one of several shore stations on the east coast of Canada. He would listen in on German radio transmissions.

Submarines would surface from time to time to send transmissions. After interpreting it, the bearing would be taken on the submarine. Only Morse code was used. No message that he received or transmitted stands out in his memory today.

The equipment that this radio operator used was the HF/DF, high frequency direction finder, commonly known as "Huff-Duff".

The general principle was to rotate a directional aerial and note where the signal was strongest. With simple aerial design, the signal would be strongest when pointing directly towards and directly away from the source. Thus, two bearings from different positions were usually taken, and the intersection plotted.

There were three or four types of messages transmitted. They could clearly be distinguished. The Barred E was a sighting report, a very short message.

The WW was a weather report. He cannot recall what a Barred B was. He does not recall having intercepted a U-257 transmission.

Bud was born in Montreal, Quebec, on January 31, 1921. He took his basic training at Montreal. He was drafted to sea from St. John's, Newfoundland.

He served on HMCS *Prestonian*, a frigate, and HMCS *Waskesiu*. For him, the food on *Waskesiu* was fair and edible.

He did not mind sleeping in a hammock. It was a matter of becoming used to it. It was comfortable, but not as much as a real bed. He took the rolls under the rafters with the movement of the waves.

He had no occasion to visit sick bay and meet the medical officer. Thus, he did not know about that officer's duties.

Life aboard the ship could be categorized by working, eating, and sleeping. Thus, he did not mix with many of the crew members, especially those doing a different type of work.

However, he was in close touch with one Oerlikon gunner as their posts were near to each other. During the battle with U-257, he directed the depth charges to the depth rail. He remembered calling, although probably not being heard, to his friend during the firing on U-257, "Let them have it!" After the war, the two sailors kept in touch.

Bud described a depth charge as being like an oil drum in appearance, although about three-quarters as tall and of similar diameter. In fact, they were often called "oil drums". When one was needed, Bud and two or three other seamen would hoist them from the ammunition locker to the railings for dropping into the water.

He was never on shore patrol or on duty watch. Ordinary seamen were assigned to duty watch. Communication personnel were required to work their posts only.

Like other seamen, there was always fear of a torpedo hitting their ship. Although there were close encounters, *Waskesiu* was never hit.

He had a brother and a sister who were in the army. His brother was stationed in Canada only.

While his sister was talking to the captain of the merchant ship *Bayano* on which she was being transported overseas, she mentioned that her brother was in the Royal Canadian Navy. When he asked the name of his ship, she said that it was *Waskesiu* but she had no idea where it was. The captain pointed to a ship that was escorting the convoy and stated that her brother was on it.

Waskesiu was assigned to escort various conveys. The escorting warships were known as a striking force. USS *Bayano*, which was transporting army signal men and CWACs, docked at Gourock, Scotland.

His sister went by train to London, where she was being stationed. Bud and his sister met later in London when on leave.

On another leave, he and two other crew members decided to go to Coventry, which they knew had been hard hit by German air attacks. They were able to witness the devastation which was rained on that Midlands city.

He spoke of the German V-1 buzz bombs, also known as "doodlebugs", that were aimed at England. One of these erratic bombs came close to him once. Shrapnel was embedded in the platform around one of the Oerlikon guns on *Waskesiu*.

He was most joyful to be home at the end of the war. He had been away from his family for four years. Upon his discharge, he returned to Montreal, where he met his wife Joan. They were married in 1952 and are still together.

His lasting impressions were seeing other countries and how they lived through the war. For example, the leave when *Waskesiu* was at Murmansk was unique for him. He has pictures of the crew on the jetty shoveling snow. Wherever they went, the crew decided to stay together as they did not know what might happen in this unfamiliar land.

For his service, he received the 1939-1945 Atlantic Star and the Canadian Volunteer Service War Medal 1939-1945.

After the war, Bud was an equipment installer for Canadian National Railways.

Bud currently lives in Maple Ridge, British Columbia.

18

Bruce Menzies

Bruce learned about the barter system in Russia. How did he fare? One day in Vancouver, Lt. Harvey took a group of Russian clients to Stanley Park, where Bruce was working at the gate of HMCS *Discovery*. In the course of talking, they learned that Bruce had been on the Murmansk Run. They were interested in knowing what his impressions of Russia were. His story emerged.

As he and a few others tried to buy something when in a Russian port, they discovered that bartering was the system for exchange of goods. This came as a shock.

However, they tried to make deals with the women from the Russian boats. Bruce exchanged a sweater for about 10,000 rubles. That, he felt, was a good deal.

When there was a request for socks, he scurried eagerly to his ship and snatched a pair of his colleague's socks that he found draped at the end of a hammock. This was traded for 10,000 more rubles. What a haul he had made with so little effort!

On the way back to England, the men played a dice game to collect each other's rubles. On arrival in England, they had acquired a duffel bag full of paper rubles. They felt very lucky. They were millionaires!

They decided to go to a bank to see how much this stash was worth. A Bank of England officer took them and their Russian money to a private room to have it counted.

As it was in progress, the sailors were thinking how lucky they were to back in England alive after such a dangerous mission. Thus, they were going to have a party that night, using some of this fortune. They had other plans for its use, as well.

The bank officer separated the denominations into three piles, counting each bill by hand over a period of about an hour. The sailors excitedly awaited the result!

Then came the electrifying news. The officer calmly stated that each pile was worth about one English pound. The men almost fainted; they were devastated! They could not believe what they heard. Was this really true?

One fellow had thrown dice for seven days and had a sore hand as a result. He did all that to find out that the money was almost worthless? The bubble had burst! They had been duped by those Russian women.

After hearing the account, one of the Russian clients pulled out his wallet and handed Bruce a Russian coin which he said was worth ten Canadian dollars. This was his consolation prize. This disenchanted sailor has kept the coin as a souvenir, fearing that it, too, might be of little monetary value.

What is the moral of this story? Never barter for goods with Russian women.

Bruce, RCNVR #V44508, was born in Montreal on July 26, 1924. In his earlier years, he spent time in a boys' brigade.

In order to enter the service earlier than the minimum age, he altered his birth certificate to show that he was older than he actually was. It worked! He took his basic training in Montreal, Cornwallis, and Halifax. He was in the navy from 1941 to 1945, with two and one-half years aboard HMCS *Waskesiu*.

After his basic training, his first service was with HMCS *Sarnia*, a minesweeper, which worked from New York to Halifax to Sydney, Nova Scotia.

He was transferred to HMCS *Amherst*, a corvette, which worked back and forth from Sydney to Newfoundland, helping to protect convoys. He spent about six months on each ship. Then he was transferred to *Waskesiu*.

Bruce and his fellow sailors would say that *Waskesiu* was a lucky, good, clean, and happy ship. In order to be a happy crew, the food had to be good. Since the food was good, everyone was happy. He felt that the ship was blessed with good cooks.

The men would pitch in and help during their watches. For instance, the night watch of 12:00 to 4:00 in the morning would prepare coffee and bacon for breakfast.

For him, it was easy to be a cook on board. He would open a can of tomatoes and empty the contents into a dish. Then, he would add bacon. If there were sausage available, this also would be added. This mixture would be allowed to stew for two hours.

The sailors referred to the recipe as red-leg bacon. When the crew would for come for breakfast, someone would ladle some of it into a dish for them. Hardtack was added next to soak it up.

For sleeping, each sailor had his own hammock. However, petty officers and higher ranks slept in bunks in small cabins.

After he became used to sleeping in a hammock, Bruce felt that he obtained his best sleeping ever. He noted that his body curved with shape of the hammock.

To enter it, he would climb onto the bulkhead, grab a bar, and pull himself up. It was like doing push-ups—not difficult at all. He experienced no trouble in either mounting or dismounting his hammock. In his opinion, any sailor who did not enjoy this way of sleeping had to have something mentally wrong with him.

After docking at Londonderry following thirty or more days at sea, two watches would go ashore while one stayed on board. Some of the onshore sailors would meet the Wrens. Others would head to a bar, where everyone was welcomed.

Eventually, the men would have some food. It would be very busy there with five ships having two hundred men on each coming in. The bar staff did not mind catering to so much business.

For food, there would be such items as bagels, sausages, chips, and duck eggs. Apparently, chicken eggs were not available. These had a better taste than the duck eggs. Bruce suspected that there must have been some sawdust in the sausages. After eating, many of the men would attend an all-night dance that featured an orchestra.

Ships were coming in almost every day. It would take about one week to complete the stocking of each— two days of which were necessary for taking food aboard. These supplies were to last for one month.

While all this was being carried out, some of the men had a rambunctious time in the city, giving shore patrol nightmares at night. Each ship, including *Waskesiu*, provided six to ten men for this duty. They would walk together along the streets. If they came across a fight, they would use their billies to break it up.

If there were a leave of two weeks, the crew might go to London. The first trip for Bruce was a new experience since he had never been there. The men would travel by ferry—hoping that there were no enemy submarines nearby—and then by train.

They stayed overnight at the Maple Leaf Club in London after visiting a local pub. They slept in triple-deck bunks. Early the next morning, a woman came in and beat the frame of each bunk. Since the men were still in a state of inebriation, this action felt like an electrocution to them. It was time to rise and leave. How they would have loved an extra hour of sleep!

Bruce and one of his pals paid a visit to Bruce's brother, a soldier at a base near Brighton, just south of London. When the men were taken to the mess hall, the cook offered them something to eat. Being hungry, they happily accepted the invitation. The cook brought each a large roast beef sandwich which they eagerly devoured.

From there, they went to visit Bruce's aunt, who lived nearby. After a visit to the local pub, they returned for a bite to eat. Just as they were about to commence, the wailing sound of air raid siren filled the room. Everyone was instructed to crawl under the big table quickly.

Bruce declined as he wanted to see the action. As he opened the door, a bomb exploded in the street. It did not take Bruce long to join the others in the tight quarters for safety beneath the kitchen table. He also learned that the British shore patrol was very strict during an air raid.

On one leave, Bruce recalled that the padre went with the ratings. However, before disembarking, he removed his white collar and his jacket, which had a cross on it to signify that he was a padre. He borrowed the jacket of a lieutenant, which had two rings on each sleeve. Now, he would be recognized as a junior officer with his men. All enjoyed their shore leave.

In 1944, *Waskesiu* returned to Nova Scotia for refitting. Bruce met his girlfriend. What a happy reunion that was after three years of being apart! They were married on December 23 of that year. The young couple then departed on a long tour. He took his bride to Shelburne while *Waskesiu* was there. When he had to leave, she returned to Montreal.

It was one year longer before he could meet the rest of his family, with the exception of his brother, who had been stationed at Brighton, England.

His lasting impression of the war is the sinking of U-257. When his fellow shipmates meet, this is a particular item of discussion.

Remembrance Day 2002 was special for Bruce and shipmate Cliff Adams. In the company of Philip Owen, mayor of Vancouver, and Iona Campanolo, Lieutenant-Governor of British Columbia, the ship's company of HMCS *Discovery* and naval veterans joined to receive an "up spirits" proclamation from the unit's commanding officer, Lt.-Cdr. King Wan. The event recognized the 50th anniversary of Her Majesty's coronation.

To mark the occasion, commemorative copper cups were made and distributed to each of the participants. Somehow, Bruce received cup #330/400. He thought that this was a coincidence since 330 was the number on the hull of *Waskesiu*.

Afterwards, the two former shipmates were invited to the unit's Seaman's Mess, where they were invited to assist the lieutenant-governor in cutting a ribbon leading to "Veteran's Corner", a section of the Seaman's Mess featuring wartime photos of Canadian ships and— most prominently—*Waskesiu*. They were honoured and it made them feel very special.

The current survivors keep in touch with each other. They have a list of names, addresses, and birthdates. Whenever anyone has a birthday anniversary, each member is supposed to telephone that person to wish him a happy birthday.

Bruce recalls that Bernard Talwin entertained his fellow crew members with his playing of the banjo and harmonica. Other than Bernard, the crew was not very musical.

On a beautiful day in 1999, Bruce was one of about 300 guests to board HMCS *Vancouver*, one of Canada's sophisticated frigates, at Canada Place on Vancouver's waterfront. He had not been on one since World War II.

The young crew members took great pride in their ship and escorted their guests around the ship, taking time to answer countless questions. They were shown such places as the bridge, the messes, engineering spaces, combat centre, and other interesting areas.

The Canadian naval sailors can perform their tasks so quickly and efficiently. The use of computers is what impressed Bruce most, reminding him of *Star Trek* – quite different from the 1940s.

The amount and quality of food offered were appreciated by all. The banyan on the flight deck was shared by both the crew and guests, allowing the guests an opportunity to talk to the young sailors representing the city of Vancouver.

The day sail lasted from 9:30 AM to 4:00 PM. A special treat occurred when the captain had the ship accelerate from 0 knots to 30 knots (35 mph, 56 km/h) in only ninety seconds. The tight turns caused many to wonder if the ship would roll over.

The old veterans really appreciated this opportunity to see a modern frigate. How Bruce would like to have been a sailor on that ship!

He was back aboard another frigate, HMCS *Regina*, in Vancouver harbour on March 9, 2007. The ship was made accessible to the public viewing. Perhaps no one was more excited than Bruce. Derek Richer wrote up his visit and the information here was gleaned from that writing.

Bruce marvelled how the weaponry and the computers outdated the equipment on *Waskesiu* during World War II. Nevertheless, he was elated that many naval traditions had not changed.

Among the guests were Lieutenant-Governor of Saskatchewan, Honourable Dr. Gordon Barnhart, and his wife. They were in attendance because of this ship's connection with their province. Both Dr. Barnhart and Commander Yvan Couture, the ship's captain, addressed the visitors.

Everyone was given a tour of the ship by Lieutenant Noonan. On the bridge, Bruce was pleased to examine one of six Browning .50-calibre machine guns, which he knew from his navy days. He was also amazed that the ship's wheel and engine telegraph resemble computer modules.

Later, at the helicopter hangar, there was more equipment to examine. A particular highlight came when Bruce held an MP5 and a shotgun for photographs. To end a dream cruise, Bruce exchanged sea stories with Lt. Noonan.

Bruce has said that, after all these years and what he had experienced, he would return to navy life if it were possible. For him, this saying is true: Once a sailor, always a sailor!

Bruce received two medals from the Russian government for work on the dangerous mission of escorting convoys to Murmansk. The British Minister of Defence issued the Arctic Star to any sailor having served on the Murmansk Run. This included those who served on merchant ships. The recipients were mainly British as there were few Canadian ships which took part.

Bruce finally received his medal—quite belatedly —in November 2007. This was probably given at that time because the Russian government had obtained permission to decorate the Canadians after the Cold War.

Often people ask Bruce how *Waskesiu* was able to accomplish so much and to escape the German U-boats and bombers. He replies that she was a clean, happy, and efficient ship. Anyone who has the time at the gate to HMCS *Discovery*, and Bruce is not busy, will likely hear some of those stories of adventure on board HMCS *Waskesiu.*

Bruce currently lives in Vancouver, British Columbia.

19

Walter Ritchie

Four German prisoners from the submarine U-257 were rescued from the water and brought aboard *Waskesiu*. Walter was one of the reception committee. Who were these enemy sailors? What kind of young men were they? He soon found out.

It was his responsibility to remove their wallets and give them to the captain of his ship. In the process, he looked inside each. What he saw had an immediate impact on him. He made sure that his feeling did not show on his face.

He removed pictures—pictures of a girlfriend, a wife, a mother, a dad. They were just like him and his fellow crew members. This experience had a sobering effect. The situation could have been the other way around. He could be submitting himself to the enemy. He wondered, if that had happened, how would he have wanted to be treated?

On return to Londonderry, the British marines arrived on board, blindfolded the prisoners, who then left for prisoner-of-war camps.

Some of the prisoners became friends with the crew. It was very evident at the ship's reunion years later when Waldemar Nickel and his wife Carmen joined the Canadians at Picton, Ontario.

When George Devonshire and his wife Phyllis hosted a super reunion, his wife Denise met Carmen, Waldemar's wife, setting the stage for a wonderful friendship. To the surprise of Walter and Denise, on June 6, 1997, Waldemar telephoned from Germany to congratulate them on their 50th wedding anniversary.

"Prisoners become lifetime friends." Walter's kind treatment of those four sailors had not been forgotten.

Walter was born in Winnipeg on December 27, 1920. He served in the navy from May 1940 to November 1945, being away from his family for five and one-half years.

He took his basic training at Esquimalt for the gunnery branch. On the west coast, he served on HMCS *Wolf* and HMCS *Lockeport*. In the Atlantic, he served on HMCS *Waskesiu* and HMCS *Prince Rupert*.

HMCS *Waskesiu*, being the first frigate in the Royal Canadian Navy, was the envy of all as it pulled into Esquimalt harbour from the shipyard. Her crew, experienced North Atlantic sailors, had arrived from the east coast.

At the time, Walter, petty officer QR1 gunnery instructor, was on Captain "D" staff with the gunnery officer, Lt. Eric Mickofsky. They were aboard K330 instructing the gunnery people and inspecting the armament.

They were "drooling" as they toured the ship and completed gun drills with the crew. The question was "How could anyone be lucky enough to be drafted on board K330?"

He was living out of barracks at the time. To Walter's surprise the next morning on arrival at the office, the gunnery officer said, "Ritchie, get a taxi and all of your gear. You're on *Waskesiu*!"

The story was that, after the party the previous night, the gunner's mate on board had climbed up the mast and out onto the yard arm—a very dangerous act —and was yelling, "High, Ho Silver!"

The yard arm is a spar near the top of a mast and projects each way at right angles. The ropes from it to the top of the mast form a triangle.

The charge laid was "Conduct not becoming of a senior petty officer. Therefore, he was off and Walter was on. How lucky could a person be! The Captain "D" gunnery officer was very envious of him at that point.

Within hours, he set sail on the start of his two years aboard *Waskesiu*—a very lucky and wonderful ship.

Just as they left harbour on the first trip out of Halifax on the Atlantic Ocean, the chief stoker, an old hand, informed him, "Well, son, this is hell." Thus, Walter was prepared for a very unpleasant experience.

At sea, the captain advised him that his position would be on the bridge to control any gunnery action. He was surprised as this duty is normally performed by a commissioned officer. However, as a petty officer, he was placed in charge of gunnery since the lieutenant in charge was college-trained, but not experienced at sea.

Officers usually were university graduates. They boarded ship totally inexperienced. They were given training, but no sea time. Each was appointed to a position of authority on board. The captain, the navigator, and Lt. Peter Nares were the only experienced officers.

Petty officers and ratings had sea time and thus were experienced in their areas. A rating had to pass examinations and be a leading seaman for a year before becoming a petty officer. Walter had three or four years of experience and schooling before he became one.

His position on the bridge as gunnery control was very interesting and exciting with his being able to see and hear all the department heads coordinate all functions in harmony to a successful conclusion. All of the gunnery training and practice action stations were now "the real thing".

The bridge was right in front of the funnel. All navigation affairs were conducted from there. It was also above the wheel house and totally exposed to the elements.

The wireless and the radar were located there. At the time, Morse code was used in the wireless. If there were a serious situation, the captain would be notified and brought there.

The captain's cabin was located just below, also. It was close so that he could go in a minute's notice. The cabin had a little bed in it. His big cabin was located by the wardroom. When the officer of the watch felt that the captain needed to be on the bridge, he would send someone for him.

Each crew had three watches—red, white, and blue. The senior seaman of each watch would be at the wheel. When the ship entered a harbour or a canal, the coxswain—the senior non-commissioned officer—would be at the wheel. A pilot from the area would come aboard and give instructions regarding the procedure.

On one occasion, the gunnery officer told him that there would be practice action stations at 4:30 PM. To his surprise, the bell went at 4:10 PM. He told his colleagues that this was only a practice. When he arrived on the bridge, the gunnery officer told him that *Tweed* had been hit. As he looked, he saw her in a vertical position slowly sinking into the sea.

One incident in regard to the action following the sinking of U-257 stands out. The firing had ceased and the prisoners had been picked up. Suddenly, shells ricocheted off the water and passed over the heads of those on the bridge.

Walter dived behind a small divider wall with his telephone cord stretched as far as it would go. The leading signal man dived on top of him. Two others ducked behind the searchlight. What was going on?

The captain immediately radioed *Nene* to order the crew to cease firing as the enemy had been sunk. The *Waskesiu* crew was never informed why the firing had taken place. That was the closest that Walter had come to being a casualty—too close.

Then, he and Lt. Lincoln went aft to be the reception committee for the prisoners.

Walter saw a writing-up in which Prime Minister Winston Churchill said that the Murmansk Run was suicide. Yes, it was very scary for all.

On one occasion, Walter saw an airplane moving slowly above his ship. A yeoman told him that it was a German recognizance plane. It would go back to its base and the pilot would report how many ships were in the convoy, the speed that it was travelling, and other pertinent information.

Because of the dressing up and the inspection, most sailors would try anything to get out of church parade. However, everyone went to one particular parade at the beginning of June 1944, especially with an official padre aboard.

The sailors had great respect for him and his message pertaining to D-Day. Walter sensed that they needed all the help available as the next day could be very eventful. The crew was very serious and participated in the hymns and prayers that they had learned in Sunday school.

On D-Day, he watched as a large landing craft passed by *Waskesiu*. He noted the load that they carried: rifle, pack sack, and heavy boots. He compared what he saw to what his crew wore: light clothing, parka, normal footwear, and life jacket. He figured that if he would land in the water, he would likely float, whereas the soldiers would not.

He did not seem to be bothered by living on *Waskesiu*. He felt that the food was very good and that his living quarters were satisfactory.

Being a petty officer, Walter did not sleep in a hammock, but in a bunk. It was not as crowded as in the ratings' quarters since there were only twelve men. There was even a mess man to look after it.

Each man had his own individual locker. The facilities were between those for officers and those for ratings in terms of comfort.

Obtaining the mail could be difficult, depending upon the weather. When the ship carrying the mail was beside *Waskesiu*, a crew member of the latter fired the Coston gun.

This gun shot a steel rod connected to a roll of light line held by another member. This line was retrieved by a crew member on the other ship. It was then tied to a heavier line, fed through a pulley, and hauled back to *Waskesiu* with the mail bag attached. On occasion, a person would be transported in this way.

He had one shore leave that was special to him. It was a trip to meet relatives in Scotland. They were shocked when he appeared at the doors of homes. During his stay, he met aunts, uncles, and other cousins whom he was unaware of their existence. He was impressed by the hospitality shown him.

On another leave, he traveled to London and enjoyed seeing the historical places.

After VE-Day had been declared, he volunteered for the war in the Pacific. The good thing about this was that all who volunteered obtained fifty-two days of leave.

After an enjoyable stay in Winnipeg, he proceeded to Esquimalt to rejoin HMCS *Prince Rupert*, another frigate, to which he had been transferred from *Waskesiu*. The ship did not leave the harbour. The atomic bomb was dropped in Japan and the war ended.

He received from Canada the four regular commemorative medals. He also received from Russia the one for working the Murmansk Run and from Great Britain the Arctic Star.

Walter mentioned that Lt.-Cdr. Fraser obtained his sea time as an RCMP officer in the Marine Division. Both he and his predecessor, Lt.-Cdr. Macdonald, were well-liked by the men.

Like other surviving members of the crew, he noted that the exploits of *Waskesiu* were little mentioned after the war. The men had inquired of numerous sources.

His time in the navy was one which he enjoyed. He was very thankful for his time on *Waskesiu*. But he looked forward to returning to civilian life. Once back into civilian life, he worked in retail management.

Walter currently lives in Winnipeg, Manitoba.

20

Charlie Robinson

What was happening? The stokers did not know, but they found out later from those who were on deck at the time.

For some reason, *Waskesiu* had stopped in the calm water of the Bay of Biscay. When she was ready to move again, the ship would not budge. It was a worrying factor because the ship was a "sitting duck", being exposed to enemy submarines.

The cause of the problem was that, as the ship attempted to move, the weight of the cat gear attached to the line over the stern caused it to become entangled in the screws of the propeller. The cat gear was a device which attracted acoustic torpedoes.

A petty officer donned a diving suit and descended into the calm water and released the line. This was Charlie's most memorable event on the ocean.

Charlie was born in Montreal, Quebec, on April 4, 1921. He was in the navy from February 23, 1942, to November 29, 1945, with about one and one-half years between leaves. His basic training was taken in Montreal.

One day when Charlie and a few friends were exploring a field during their time in Bermuda, they entered a shed. Here they found various gardening tools.

As he was moving the soil on the floor with his foot, he located a metal object. It was a pair of British handcuffs made of tempered steel, but a bit rusty. The keys were still in the locks. He noted that to open the spring-loaded locks, he had to turn each key like a screw.

A little later in Newfoundland, while helping to load a five-gallon pail of white lead, used for making paint, he set it down without bending his knees. This resulted in his injuring his back. He was transported to hospital on a stretcher. He spent a month there lying on a board on a mattress.

When a problem arose on *Waskesiu* just after it left port, the ship returned for repairs. That made it possible for Charlie to rejoin his crew.

The living quarters aboard *Waskesiu* were good. Stokers had a mess separate from those of other seamen. It was about 15 feet by 20 feet (4.5 x 6 m), and was well kept and comfortable. He did not mind sleeping in hammocks.

The food rations were plentiful. Examples of the variety included eggs, bacon, tomatoes, meat, fish, tinned vegetables, desserts, and a tot every day. Desserts consisted of such items as canned pears or peaches, but nothing special. There was also no fresh fruit.

The mess was located in the forward part of the second deck of the ship, just below the communications deck. In front of it was the chain locker which stored the anchors. Below it was a storage area for keeping meat cold.

Behind the mess, one after the other, were the seamen's mess, a boiler room, another boiler room, the engine room, and finally the tiller flat where the steering gear was located and food supplies were stored.

Charlie worked in the engine room as a leading stoker aboard ship on two frigates, HMCS *Waskesiu* and HMCS *Annan*. He was in charge of the evaporator which made fresh water from sea water. This water was used in the boilers. After evaporation, the water was stored in tanks. From there, it was pumped into the boilers, as needed.

The ship had four-cylinder twin engines. It was necessary to keep these engines oiled. Each connecting rod had a long copper tube that connected with the bearings below.

Oil had to be poured into the cup, which was located above the tube. Since the engine was turning at 1,500 rpm, the cup was not stationary. To fill it, a sailor had to keep the same motion as the rods. From the cup, the oil went to the bearings.

To check for overheating, a sailor would place the back of his hand next to a connecting rod. If the rod became too hot, it could burn the babbits in the bearing. If that should happen, it would be necessary to pour cold, fresh water over it since it was an open bearing. As soon as the bearing was cooled, one could return to oiling it through the cups.

The boiler pressure was 225 pounds (1,550 kPa), but Charlie could not recall for sure. It was necessary to keep the gauge at that mark.

He had to be careful that the tube showing the level of water in the boiler could be read. If it were overfull, it was difficult to determine if it were empty or full. If this situation should occur, there was a certain procedure to follow to bring back the view of what the level was.

Waskesiu had a hold capacity for 750 tons of oil. The oil would be stored in several tanks. When she was refueled at sea, a tanker would sail parallel to Waskesiu and run a four-inch flexible pipe to her. A line would be dropped and towed onto the ship. The pipe would be connected to one of the half-dozen fittings on deck. The oil, usually crude, then would be pumped in.

When crude oil was to be used, it had to be preheated to make it thinner in order for it to run through the lines on the ship easily. Otherwise, it would be like jelly. This was a problem in cold weather as would be the case in mid Atlantic and the Arctic.

Occasionally, fuel oil would be pumped aboard. This was preferable as it burned more easily. Most of the refueling was accomplished in the Bay of Biscay since the weather was warmer.

The stokers had a unique way of tending to their laundry, unlike other crew members. There were pumps in the boiler room. Each had a valve for releasing steam.

A man would place some soft soap into a bucket and add his dirty laundry. Then, he would shoot steam into the bucket to keep the water boiling. He would use a stick to move the laundry in the bucket back and forth until it would be clean.

Other sailors would bring their hammocks to the boiler room to be scrubbed prior to officers' inspection. They were charged one shilling by the stokers to do the work. The gear would be set onto the floor of the heads. There, it would be scrubbed with soft soap and hosed down. Then, they were ready for inspection in the mess decks.

Charlie has a few memories of his visit to Russia. At this time of year, there was daylight for twenty-four hours a day.

The place on Kola Inlet where *Waskesiu* docked was about twenty-five miles from Murmansk. There were a number of small boats with women soldiers aboard. He noticed that an older woman seemed to be always on the jetty. Some of the fellows had their pictures taken with her.

Also on the jetty was a 1929 Ford pickup truck which had been converted from using gasoline to using diesel. It had a four-cylinder engine without a fuel pump. It had little buckets on the connecting rods. As the rods went down, they picked up oil and threw it onto the bottom of the pistons to lubricate them.

At the time of the invasion of Europe, LTC boats carried the troops across the English Channel to France. On the return trip, some would pull up beside

Waskesiu. The sailors would scrounge food brought back by the boats.

One time the sailor on lookout saw something floating on the water. Therefore, the ship moved along side it to pick it up. It was the body of a German sailor. He still had his uniform on, but the exposed parts of his body were like a skeleton.

The body was brought on board and searched. His wallet, containing pictures of his family, was found and turned over to the British authorities. The body was wrapped in canvas, which was then sewn up and weighted. Then the sailor was given a proper burial at sea.

If it were a warm day in the Bay of Biscay, Charlie would strip to the waist and lie in the sun on the deck when off duty. However, he kept his life jacket close at hand.

Like the other survivors, he is concerned that so little has been written about *Waskesiu.* This ship sailed into numerous ports in about fourteen countries.

After the war, Charlie spent the first year taking life easy at the home of his parents. Jobs at that time were very scarce because of the increase in the work force. He eventually obtained a position with Northern Telecom, where he stayed for thirty years.

Charlie currently lives in Wasaga Beach, Ontario.

21

Allan Tustian

It was a most disastrous and heart-rending experience! *Waskesiu* was sailing beside *Nene* and *Tweed*. Allan was at his action station reading the radar and monitoring all ships within range as there were submarines in the area.

Suddenly, one ship disappeared from the screen! She had been only one or two miles away. Where did it go? He informed the bridge that he had lost the ship.

The disheartening reply came back that the ship had been sunk very quickly. That was *Tweed*. He could only think of the loss of crew members, of which he learned there were many.

Allan was born in Kagawong, on Manitoulin Island, Ontario. The place where he lives now is about 15 miles (24 km) from where he grew up. Both places are beside lakes with the same names as the communities.

His time in the navy was from August 1941 to October 1945. He took his basic training at HMCS *York*, in Toronto and served at HMCS *Stadacona*, in Halifax, on HMCS *St. Francis*, HMCS *Timmins*, and HMCS *Waskesiu*.

On entering the service, he and another fellow were not sure what they wanted for a specialty. Eventually, they decided to take RDS—Radio Data System. This turned out to be radar, a new technology developed by the British just before the war.

For training, they were sent to a little place near Halifax for a two-week period. The practical aspect amounted to not much more than turning the set on and off.

When the courses had been completed, Allan was drafted onto HMCS *St. Frances.* He became one of three operators aboard. On *Waskesiu*, he was in charge of six radar operators.

The instrument which he used did not have an antenna, but was set at a 45° angle. It was able to determine ranges and distances. The set was very small, about six inches (15 cm) across, giving a very small picture. It also had a cathode ray tube something like that of a television set. It was very crude compared with what was available five years later. One of Allan's friends invented some of the parts.

With himself and the writer, there were eight men of his crew, in addition to the other ratings, living in an area of 30 feet by 10 feet (9 x 3 m). That was not much room in which to live for three years.

Everyone slept in hammocks in these small quarters in the mess hall. When in the hammock, one did not move because the hammock moved with the ship. It was very comfortable.

The writer in this group was responsible for keeping the data of what transpired aboard ship. There were more than one writer, but Allan worked with the head writer.

He felt that the food on *Waskesiu* was better than on his other ships and very good when compared with army rations. There was almost a mutiny on the high seas when some crew members of his first ship, HMCS *St. Frances*, expressed their objection over the quality of the food being served.

At the time of the sinking of U-257, his duty was to be on the radar set at action stations. When the submarine surfaced, it was still dark and he was able to give direction and range for the gunners.

Everyone became used to rough seas, although some sailors would become sick. Allan had little trouble with sea sickness. It was difficult during meals as it would be necessary to hang onto everything on the table with both hands lest the dishes skirt suddenly to another part of the table.

It was more difficult for outside watch than for inside watch. Those sailors who were outside became drenched most of the time. That is why some of the gear was kept in the wet room.

Allan's watch was mainly at the radar sets. He did have outside watch on a corvette and a destroyer, but he had no crow's nest watch. He also was assigned as a navigator yeoman. The position was like being an assistant through which he could learn the work from the navigator.

Allan had at least two wonderful leaves in London. However, his most impressive leave was in Scotland. He found that the people were wonderful and wanted to do as much as possible for the service personnel.

He stayed in a private home with a family. However, he found it very cold as heating was accomplished only by fireplaces. There was no central heating. It was necessary for him to bundle himself in extra clothing all the time to avoid "freezing". The people in the home were used to this form of heating. Despite the cold, he was very appreciative of the hospitality extended to him.

Visiting a little Russian town when *Waskesiu* made her trip to Murmansk was an eye-opener. What a very desolate place it was! Most of the houses were wooden, but the hospital was brick.

He and a friend proceeded to the top of a hill and gazed into the valley on the other side. Below them was a train being hauled by an immense steam locomotive. Also, streaming before them was a non-ending single file of men. Who they were and why they were there were mysteries to the Canadians.

During their tour, they were careful not to go out-of-bounds. Seeing armed guards protecting areas where foreigners were forbidden was sufficient deterrent.

He enjoyed being a sailor. On occasion, he was the mailman when *Waskesiu* docked at a port as he usually was the first man off the ship.

On one occasion, he was unable to reach his ship for a couple of days. In the interim, he spent his time on a couple other ships. While waiting one time, he saw General Eisenhower and his secretary pass by. He found that to be impressive.

Being aboard *Waskesiu*, which he felt had the best crew of any with whom he sailed, provided Allan with his most lasting memory. An efficient team effort made it easier for him and his fellow crew members. The officers were very capable and all performed their jobs to the best of their ability.

He was at home on three leaves, each of which was for twenty-eight days, in five years. .He left the ship in Victoria in June 1945. Since he had volunteered for the war against Japan, he was given a 60-day leave and went home. Because the war ended in August, he was discharged in the following October.

He was awarded all of the service medals issued to the crew. In later years, he received the Murmansk medal and the Arctic Star.

After the war, Allan, like many others, did not know what he would do for his future. At first, he stayed with his sister and her husband, who had a tourist resort called Treasure Isle beside a lake on Manitoulin Island, in Lake Huron. She invited him to work there as she needed the help. He agreed to stay for one year. However, this became his life's work.

Allan currently lives in Mindemoya, Ontario.

22

Roy Venner

Probably the duty which he would least like doing again would be the rescuing of someone in the water, especially in the dark.

In the case of U-257, the frigate had been chasing it for several hours on a moonless night. When it was finally sunk, there were several German sailors in the water.

There were tricky manoeuvres to perform from the time of the launching until the boat and sailors were aboard the ship again. It was a skilled operation to launch an oar-powered wooden boat from the ship. Roy stated that he came out well, despite the danger.

One particular danger in such a rescue was always present. If a rescue boat were to come upon several sailors in a group and all tried to board it at the same time, the boat very likely would capsize, throwing everyone into the water.

Leslie Roy was born in Long Branch, Ontario, on July 1, 1923. He took his basic training at HMCS *York*, in Toronto, and then served at HMCS *Naden*, land base in Victoria. Later, he served on HMCS *Waskesiu*, HMCS

Ontario (light cruiser), and on HMCS *Caraquit* (minesweeper). Between 1942 and 1945, he served as a seaman.

When he was at HMCS *York* following his enlistment, the base was located on the Canadian National Exhibition grounds. The automotive building served as a barracks. Later, a new base was established along the Toronto waterfront.

He did not specialize in any aspect of the ship's duties; and, therefore, he had to be prepared to do any task. Sometimes, he was a lookout and, sometimes, he was an after gunner. One of his important tasks was to aid in the rescue of men in the water.

He occasionally had to transport the medical officer from *Waskesiu* to another ship. He would remain on the other ship until the doctor had completed his work. Then he would transport him back to his own ship.

On one occasion, he was required to transport the medical officer on a bos'n chair via a tight line to a large merchant ship that had drawn up beside the smaller *Waskesiu*. It was necessary that *Waskesiu* and the other ship keep an even course and speed against the wave action so that the wire would not dip into the water or tighten too much and snap. It was a tricky manoeuver. The doctor had been called to perform an appendectomy on a merchant sailor.

He found living quarters to be crowded—but he shared them with fine guys. Hammocks were about two feet wide when made up. They were so close that they would touch those of their ship mates. Although there were a few flaws, he was able to manage.

One fellow near him was where a row of beds were. If waves should come into the mess hall where he was sleeping, he would need to bale out of his hammock. In such a case, he was not a happy sailor.

There was chapel service on Sunday mornings as often as they could be carried out. However, Roy has lost memory of them. Besides these services, the padre had other functions. An important one was being a morale booster to the sailors.

He also helped in the censoring of letters that the sailors wrote to family and friends back home. It was very important that no secrets be given out in the time of war.

He was happy that he never had to do shore patrol. The bigger and older sailors had that responsibility. There was an exciting time in one place just before the ship left port. Some cooks had been in trouble with shore patrol when on leave. They decided to even the score with shore patrol. Thus, they went ashore to encounter them. They accomplished their goal. However, it resulted in their spending some time in the brig for their misbehaviour.

During the battle with the submarine, he was on the #2 four-inch gun, which helped put the finishing touches to the conning tower.

Everyone on board seemed to enjoy dancing. Whenever they were on shore leave, they would search out a dance hall. One of their favourite places in this respect was Londonderry. The sailors particularly liked this city, especially since they were respected by the people. The citizens looked forward to their return to their city.

It was different with Halifax. Roy figured that some service personnel wanted to make matters even with the city for something considered to have been wrong. Such action did not seem to be of much sense. He happened to have been at sea when the riots took place.

He feels that the crew was a lucky gang many times, but always together, afraid of nothing. There were events in which he participated of which he would be afraid to do today. Like his fellow seamen, he feels that *Waskesiu* had a good crew. Everyone was proud of everyone else.

Roy had a particular friend on board, a big, young fellow from Newfoundland. He was described as a real Newfie sailor. The two worked together on various jobs.

On returning home after the war, there was nothing but happiness—and no job. However, he eventually became a millwright and machinist.

Roy attended the reunion at Pinyer's Cove, Ontario, a very impressive event. Although a few of the men had met each other at other times, it meant much to Roy after so many years since they had worked together on *Waskesiu*.

Roy currently lives in Mississauga, Ontario.

23

Art Wall

The rations on board Canadian ships were adequate, but sparse in most cases, especially on Fairmile Q055, as Art recalled. He related one example.

The cook would order supplies when the ship was in a port. In the matter of grapefruit, he would order nine for a crew of eighteen. That meant one-half of a grapefruit per man for one meal only.

However, when his crew was on loan to the United States Navy, those nine grapefruit became nine cases of them! The crew did not know where to put so many on their small ship. He had no such recollection for *Waskesiu*.

Art was born at Gateshead-on-Tyne, England, on May 25, 1922. He joined the navy just prior to his eighteenth birthday in May 1940 and served until 1945. He took his basic training at Halifax, after which he served in the Seamen Branch as a gun layer on HMCS *Nootka*, a minesweeper; HMCS Fairmile ML Q055, a motor launch; and HMCS *Waskesiu*.

Spending that first summer at HMCS *York*, in Toronto, doing boring guard work duty certainly was not exciting. Matters improved when he was drafted to HMCS *Stadacona*, in Halifax, on August 22.

By November 12, he had completed his training as a gun layer. Sea time came two days later when he was drafted to HMCS *Nootka*, one of the minesweepers operating daily out of Halifax. (Her name was changed to HMCS *Nanoose* in 1943 so that her original name could be given to a *Tribal* class destroyer.)

On April 7, 1941, Art was promoted to the rank of able seaman, and on April 21, 1942, he became part of the crew of the Fairmile ML Q055. On this ship, he served out of Halifax, Sydney, and Gaspé, along with eleven other Fairmiles, until January 1, 1943. Q055 was 118 feet long (36 m) and had a twin Packard engine which allowed the boat to travel 20 knots (23 mph, 37 km/h).

When the United States Navy was having trouble with convoys in the Gulf of Mexico and the Caribbean Sea, it asked the Canadian government for help.

Two flotillas of Fairmiles were sent from Halifax. When they arrived in the harbour at Jacksonville, Florida, the first eleven ran over a submerged object, which knocked off the ASDIC dome. Q055, on which Art served, was not damaged. Because of all the damage making them inoperable, the ships were sent back to Halifax.

Then he was drafted to HMCS *Givenchy*, in Esquimalt, with fourteen days leave en route to become part of the crew of HMCS *Waskesiu*. While waiting for her completion, he took courses to become a leading seaman and petty officer.

On June 16, 1943, Art stowed his hammock on
Waskesiu. Just prior, the gunners' mate did something
improper and was transferred off the ship. Walter
Ritchie, who was in the gunnery department at
Esquimalt, was transferred to the ship as a replacement,
arriving on the same day that Art arrived.

After trials, the ship left for Halifax via the Panama
Canal. On the way, there was a stop at Bermuda. The
crew decided to celebrate Art's achieving promotion in
rank at Esquimalt recently. They managed to have him
intoxicated in the process.

Finally, the ship arrived in Londonderry. He feels
that *Waskesiu* was fortunate in spending most of her
entire commission there because Canadian ships in
Canadian and Newfoundland bases often suffered loss
of part of their crew as the more experienced members
were drafted to newly constructed ships.

This did not happen to *Waskesiu* in Londonderry.
Thus, her crew remained together and became a happy,
efficient, and well-trained crew.

Regarding his personal role in the sinking of
U-257, he was the gun layer on the after-gun on the
quarterdeck of *Waskesiu*. It was necessary to wait until
the submarine came into view around the forward
superstructure, and then fire star shells to illuminate
the sky. Their point of aim was the conning tower and
the forward gun, giving her crew no opportunity to fire
on *Waskesiu*.

He said that the gun which he operated, a product
of Massey-Harris, was a poor model. Its discharge

achieved a velocity of 1,100 feet per second (335 m/s). The shells were visible as they passed through the air because of their low velocity. Nevertheless, it served its purpose well since it put two holes into U-257.

Art's gun was assigned to *Waskesiu* as a star shell gun. The star shell was designed to explode and to create much light at the point of explosion. In action against U-257, the gun was fired to light up an area with star shells. It actually lit up about one-third of the 360° horizon before switching to armour-piercing shells. The shells seemed to be suspended parachutes as they gently floated to the surface of the water.

On the Murmansk Run, the convoy included the cruiser USS *Milwaukee*, which was being turned over to the Russian Navy under the Lend-Lease programme.

There were a number of submarine contacts. On one occasion a torpedo hit the cat gear of *Waskesiu*. The cat gear was towed behind the ship. It was a couple of bars separated by a half-inch of steel and towed as a bridle. The bars were 36 inches (91 cm) long and separated so that, when the water passed between them, they rattled. It was programmed so that this rattling effect attracted acoustical torpedoes.

On arrival, the American crew allowed the Canadians to board *Milwaukee* to purchase anything from their well-stocked canteen. The Canadians readily took advantage of this.

However, as soon as the ship had been turned over to the Russians and the Americans had left, no one, including the Americans, was allowed aboard. This ended the opportunity for the Canadians to purchase rations.

Art found the Russians very friendly and eager to receive anything that the Canadians presented to them. They were very hard up for rations.

At the conclusion of the war, there was near-rioting in Halifax. All liquor stores were closed. Fortunately, *Waskesiu* was still at sea when this event occurred. Therefore, its crew did not participate.

Servicemen created much damage in the city. Art feels that, in a way, they had some justification for doing this. Authorities and the population of Halifax seemed to have a dislike for all servicemen and did not treat them well. It was a completely different situation in Sydney, Nova Scotia, and St. John's, Newfoundland, where servicemen—especially those in the navy—were treated with much respect.

On his return to Canada in 1945, Art volunteered for the Pacific. Since the navy was accepting only unmarried personnel, he was released and returned to civilian life.

It was his intention to attend university in Toronto to become an engineer. At that time, his brother was attending teachers' college and recommended Art to do the same. The incentive was that it took four years to become an engineer before being able to earn a living. However, it took one year to be a teacher, and, thus, receive an earlier income.

He accepted the logic and entered teachers' college in Toronto and spent the next thirty years as a teacher in Toronto's schools. He has never regretted his decision. Because of his war service, he was able to retire at age fifty-five. As of this writing, he is still enjoying that retirement.

The memory that stands out most is the wonderful friends whom he made. It was quite hard when he lost a couple of them. He would like to say that he enjoyed the time which he spent in the navy, especially on *Waskesiu* with a great group of guys.

During the two years on *Waskesiu* and as a petty officer, there was only one of the crew whom he had to put "in the rattle"—and that guy was "our very own Bruce Menzies!"

Art currently lives in Haliburton, Ontario.

24

Waldemar (Peter) Nickel

Much of this account is taken from a letter dated March 11, 1998, from Waldemar Nickel to Robert Hodgkinson and forwarded to George Devonshire.

From May to the end of August in 1943, Waldemar passed through the *Marine-Nachrichten-Schule* [Naval Intelligence School] at Flensburg, training in wireless traffic, code, and decode with the Enigma code machine Enigma; the *Torpedo-Schule* [Torpedo School] at Flensburg, with practice-firing on the Baltic Sea off Travemünde; a short course about the new acoustic torpedo T5 at Gotenhafen; and the Anti-Aircraft School at Swinemünde, with shooting on the Baltic Sea.

He joined the crew of U-257, under *Kapitanleutnant* Heinz Rahe, in September 1943 at Lorient, France. The submarine had returned from her fourth patrol at the end of August 1943 for repairs, having operated in the Gulf of Guinea without success.

On November 9, 1943, they left Lorient for the next patrol, escorted as far as the 200-metre-line (656 ft) water depth. As usual, U-257 submerged for a test down to 200 metres (656 ft) before the escort could be released. On this occasion, they found out that the sound detector did not work. So they had to return to St. Nazaire, France.

On January 2, 1944, they left St. Nazaire for the last patrol of U-257. Their task was to go to the southern entrance of Denmark Strait, which separates Greenland and Iceland, in the area near Cape Farewell, the southern tip of Greenland. There they were supposed to meet a German blockade runner and escort her through the Denmark Strait.

Although the submarine had to struggle against a heavy sea, it reached the meeting point according to schedule. For several days they waited, but the blockade runner did not appear.

Therefore, U-257 was allowed to operate free in that region with the order to send twice a day—in the morning before submerging for the day and in the evening after surfacing for the night—short radio messages about her position, the weather conditions, and barometer readings. The same order was given to other submarines that operated in other parts of the North Atlantic. All these data were needed for the weather forecast in Germany and other parts of Europe.

He suspected that the short radio message which U-257 had sent in the twilight of February 23, 1944, was located by HF/DF of the Sixth Escort Group. About half an hour after the radio message had gone out, they received a danger signal from their improved warning set against radio waves called Naxos. As a result, the submarine crash dived.

Because they did not hear any screw noises at the sound detector and on the supposition that it had been an aircraft, U-257 surfaced once more after about an hour. At the surface, Naxos gave immediately danger signals. Again the submarine crash dived and changed course. After a while, they heard the screw noises of *Nene* and *Waskesiu* and then the first ASDIC impulses. The struggle began.

To evade the escorts' depth charges, they changed course and speed and went down to 230 metres (755 ft). *Nene* and *Waskesiu* must have been a very good team and knew their job. After about nine hours of depth charging—singles and series up to four—U-257 was caught at a depth of 230 metres (755 ft).

The rear of the submarine was heavily damaged. A considerable amount of water had entered through several leaks. Also, the rudders were blocked. Because the submarine became too heavy and could not be held, the commanding officer gave the order to blow out the diving cells with all their compressed air. It succeeded in surfacing.

The attempt to fire an acoustic torpedo failed because the stern torpedo tube was damaged and could not be opened. When it was obvious that the situation was hopeless, the captain gave the order to abandon the ship.

Waldemar made his way to the conning tower. Because it was crowded, he climbed down to the upper deck where some of the crew were waiting. He did not see that his commanding officer had reentered the boat.

It was a new moon night and everywhere it was very dark. The two frigates alternately fired star shells and high explosive shells until U-257 sank.

When the submarine went down, Waldemar found himself in the water, which was at 8°C (46°F). He and six crew members who were near him formed a group and swam—with life-belts—to the stopped *Nene*. After about three-quarters of an hour, they reached *Nene* and climbed aboard over an outboard net which was brought out on her port side. On board, the crew treated the German survivors very fairly, almost as if they were comrades.

The POW camp at Bowmanville, Ontario, where Waldemar was a prisoner for a while, was the same camp where Commodore "Silent" Otto Kretschmer was detained. Waldemar was also detained at Seebe, a camp west of Calgary and at Wainwright, Alberta.

Later on from the end of 1945 until the repatriation of Kretschmer in the summer of 1947, he met the commodore once more at Camp Llanmartin, near Newport, England. From time to time, they played bridge in the evening.

Other members of the U-257 crew were detained at camps in the United States.

Waldemar stated that he would never forget what an officer of *Nene* said to him just before the German sailors were handed over to the army at Londonderry. "I hope that you felt happy aboard *Nene* in these circumstances. As long as your submarine swam, we were enemies. When your boat sank, you were for us shipwrecked people; and sailors all over the world will always understand. I am sure you will think just so."

After his repatriation in December 1947, Waldemar found his mother at Lübeck, Germany. His father had died in July 1944 at Stettin. He received that message from the International Red Cross at Geneva when he was at Seebe.

His mother had fled from Stettin to Lübeck some days before the Soviet army entered Stettin at the end of April 1945. She was able to save only two cases and the most important personal papers and documents. She lived in a single room of about 10 square metres.

The family could not return to Stettin, their home town and Waldemar's birthplace, because, at the Conferences of Yalta and Potsdam, parts of Eastern Germany were given to Poland as compensation for the eastern parts of Poland which the Soviet Union had annexed in 1939. Therefore, the family started at zero.

On June 3, 1950, Waldemar and Carmen were married. It was very difficult to locate a job. In an effort to earn a living, Waldemar learned to be a mason as did many former officers, and worked in that trade until March 1951. When conditions had improved in Germany, he started a new career at the German Post as a high post office clerk on April 1, 1951. Until he retired in 1987, he worked in various positions within the German Post.

As of 1998, surviving members of the crew of U-257 who were in good health had been meeting each year somewhere in Germany for the past thirty years. However, nearly every year, the group has become smaller. Sometimes, there have been more widows than ex-crew members in attendance.

On August 10, 2000, Waldemar wrote a letter to Bruce Menzies. It reads as follows:

> Dear Bruce,
>
> Hello, our dear friend and "old Waskesiu-salt". We hope you and all your family are well, as we do.
>
> We did it already by telephon [sic], but once more Carmen and I thank you so much for your good wishes to our golden wedding, the

24. Waldemar (Peter) Nickel

enclosed video copy of the Waskesiu-reunion and for the photos of you at Londonderry. Oh boy, what a very good looking seaman!

Our big day was a happy one. We spent it with all our family and some very good friends and had a good time and a lot of fun together.

We were so touched when we got the congratulations and good wishes on our golden wedding from nearly all friends, we met at Picton.

Today just one year has gone since that wonderful and unforgettable reunion at Picton. It was a very successful and emotional event not only for you and all your shipmates but also for Carmen and me.

Even if Canada is far away, our thoughts are so often very close to you and all the other vets, we met at Picton. And when we regard the video-tapes, the spontaneous embraces at the first meeting, in short, the warm welcome we have had, it seems to us as if it occured [sic] yesterday.

In the meantime our yearly U-257-meeting took place in May. But every year the number of the still living declines. This time four vets and six women had come and as you can imagine, my report on the marvellous Waskesiu-reunion and the showing of the video-tape were the highlights of our meeting.

For this time we say bye, once more thanks for your good wishes, the enclosures and we hope as you do, we'll all meet again one day.

Greetings to all your family and stay healthy.

Sincerely your friends

Peter & Carmen

On September 14, 2005, Waldemar Nickel passed away in Lübeck, Germany. A translation of his funeral notice follows.

We say goodbye to my husband, our father, my father-in-law, and my beloved dad.

Waldemar (Peter) Nickel

August 8, 1923—Stettin

September 14, 2005—Lübeck

The funeral service takes place on Thursday, 22 September 2005, at 14:15 hours in the chapel of the Castle Gate Cemetery.

24. Waldemar (Peter) Nickel

The burying of the urn takes place later in a private family ceremony.

In place of flowers we ask for a donation for the "Rickers-Kock-Haus" at the Lubecker Hospice. Note: Waldemar Nickel.

Our thanks is given to all who stood by us in our bereavement, ready to help us in any way.

La mer a bercé
mon coeur pour la vie.
Charles Trenet

Wir nehmen Abschied von meinem Mann, unserem Vater, meinem Schwiegervater und meinem geliebten Pa

Waldemar (Peter) Nickel

* 8. August 1923   † 14. September 2005
Stettin   Lübeck

Carmen Nickel geb. Meseck
Angela und Bernd Lübbing
Jens Nickel
Anne Lübbing

Lübeck, Achternhof 28

Die Trauerfeier findet am Donnerstag, dem 22. September 2005, um 14.15 Uhr in der Kapelle des Burgtorfriedhofes statt.

Die spätere Urnenbeisetzung erfolgt im engsten Familienkreis.

Anstelle freundlich zugedachter Blumen bitten wir um eine Spende für das Lübecker Hospiz "Rickers-Kock-Haus" auf das Konto 4 164 911 bei der Volksbank Lübeck, BLZ 230 90142, Stichwort: Waldemar Nickel.

Unser Dank gilt all denjenigen, die uns in schweren Stunden einfühlsam und hilfsbereit zur Seite standen.

25

Reunion at Vancouver

A small group of veterans and wives met on May 9, 1998, in the mess hall at HMCS *Discovery*. This was the first time that there had been any kind of gathering since the war ended.

For a period of two hours, the sailors exchanged photographs and reminisced of the time when they had worked together on HMCS *Waskesiu*. During this time, they also planned for the holding of a reunion near Picton, Ontario, where more veterans would be able to attend.

After that, they proceeded to the Vancouver Lawn Tennis and Badminton Club for dinner. The menu consisted of the following dishes: smoked onion bisque, California mixed greens with basil vinaigrette, roast prime rib of beef with Yorkshire puddings "au jus", bon ton diplomat cake, fresh fruit.

Those who attended included Cliff and Donna Adams, George and Phyllis Devonshire, Andy and Zina Kaija, and Bruce and Mary Menzies.

26

Reunion at Prinyer's Cove

On August 11, 1999, a few former crew members of Canadian HMCS *Waskesiu* and German U-257 met at Prinyer's Cove, near Picton, Ontario. It was fifty-five years after the crews of these two opposing ships met on the field of battle in the North Atlantic in February, 1944. They got back together to talk about the incident from their own perspectives and to hear what it was like for the other crew.

What immediately came sharply into focus was that each crew was just following orders. It was the job of U-257 to harass Allied shipping and stop vulnerable supplies from reaching the front. HMCS *Waskesiu*, on the other hand, was assigned the task of engaging any U-boats which might attack convoys.

Waldemar (Peter) Nickel, a lieutenant on U-257, remembered that the submarine was trying to avoid the *Waskesiu* attack, suffering minor damage in the initial firing of depth charges, avoiding almost completely several other attacks, but then being heavily damaged by the final attack about 5:00 that morning.

When the U-boat was knocked out of commission on the surface and began sinking, the German crew began yelling, "Hallo, Kamerad!" to rescuing crews prior to entering the water. A fellow crew member was about to yell something else to the crew of *Waskesiu* when Lt. Nickel shushed him by saying, "Save your breath; you will need it once you go in the water."

Having sunk the enemy vessel, though, the *Waskesiu* and *Nene* crew proved none of their former actions had anything personal attached to them. As vanquished enemy, the U-257 crew now became distressed mariners to be rescued from a watery grave, the fear of most sailors.

They set about pulling the survivors out of the water. Peter remembered having a lit cigarette put into his mouth almost as quickly as his feet touched the deck of HMS *Nene*. They were given warm dry clothes, hot coffee and otherwise treated with respect, even being given the opportunity to dine with their opposite numbers on the rescuing ship.

Meeting at Prinyer's Cove allowed the two crews to compare notes, to establish a friendship which developed a personal side to the event, and finally to close the books on a situation over which they had no control fifty-five years prior.

While it was not a personal thing at the time, Waldemar Nickel and George Devonshire had made it personal now. They were reunited after a former airman, Robert Hodgkinson, contacted Waldemar while trying to

gather information on another matter. Robert then contacted George.

George Devonshire and his wife Phyllis, who live in Picton, invited the surviving crew members and their wives to attend a reunion at their home. A total of twenty-five persons attended. Among them were Waldemar Nickel and his wife Carmen, who were guests in the home of the Devonshires. Speakers at the event were Bruce Menzies, George, and Waldemar.

The German guest spoke about the submarine on which he served and the battle in which it was sunk. As the depth charges were dropped, the submarine rocked and rolled, and after coming to the surface, eventually sank. The lights went out and the batteries gave out. There was nothing for her to do but come to the surface.

The men tried to shoot it out, but the *Waskesiu* shot first. When shooting became hopeless for the men in the submarine, they went overboard. The commanding officer, *Kapitänleutnant* Heinz Rahe, threw his life jacket to one of his men, then descended into the submarine and went down with it.

Two whalers from *Waskesiu* were sent out in the choppy water to try to rescue the German sailors. They picked up a few, but many could not be reached in the darkness.

George Devonshire and Waldemar Nickel had begun to correspond about a year before the reunion. It was fascinating for George to learn what it was like from the German's point of view on the receiving end of the frigate's attack.

In the newspaper accounts, Waldemar was
described as a real Nazi type. At this reunion he stated
that it does not touch him at all. He, his family, and his
friends have heartily laughed at that. It's nothing else
but propaganda. He held no grudge over the attack,
noting that they were sailors on both sides. George
spoke of his friend as a very fine gentleman.

It was a special reunion for these veterans. Their
eyes glistened with the recollection of their battle so
many years previously and the friends whom they lost
that day and in intervening years.

A dinner was held at the Waring House in Picton,
Ontario, in honour of Waldemar and his wife Carmen. It

was a truly emotional time. He thanked the Canadians for the good treatment that they had given him.

The menu was as follows: cream of roasted pepper and wild wellington mushroom soup *or* light mixed field green salad, beef tenderloin mille-feuille *or* stuffed carmelized orange chicken *or* local county fresh pickerel, fresh local county vegetables, roasted new red potatoes, dark and white chocolate mousse cake, fresh brewed coffee and tea.

Among the veterans, with their wives, in attendance were the following: Gordon Arnold, George Devonshire, Bill Gibb, Andy Kaija, Bruce Menzies, Waldemar Nickel, Harry Ruston, and Ben Webb.

27

Reunion at Waskesiu Lake

It was an emotional reunion for veterans of HMCS *Waskesiu* who visited the town which bears the name of their ship.

From Ontario to British Columbia, thirteen veterans, their spouses, and their families gathered in Waskesiu from June 13-16, 2003, for the 60th anniversary of the commissioning of HMCS *Waskesiu*, on which the men had served during World War II. The reunion was highlighted by a public remembrance service held on Sunday outside the town's Nature Centre.

About 300 people from the town, which included a large number of people born after World War II had

ended, attended the service. They paid their respect with applause for those who represented the town's name.

During the service, Aaron Burk rang the bell which sat on HMCS *Waskesiu*, in memory of the ships fallen in the Battle of the Atlantic. The bell now resides at the Prince Albert Historical Museum.

The adoration of the townspeople was felt by the veterans. They said the town had really embraced them all weekend. Cliff Adams stated that there is a link between the ship's company and the people in the whole town of Waskesiu.

He had "scouted out" the town in the previous September in preparation for the reunion. Until that time, the crew had not connected this little town with their frigate. Likewise, the townspeople had not met any of the crew before this reunion took place.

On Friday evening, the veterans, their wives, and their families had a very enjoyable time as they renewed acquaintance, met the families, and told tales, both old and new.

On Saturday, the group met some of the local townsfolk and helped celebrate the 75th anniversary of Prince Albert National Park. Since it was also the 60th anniversary for HMCS *Waskesiu*, the local liquor store had a special on one of its products.

They attended a Parks Canada showing of a *Grey Owl* film and examined displays at the Nature Centre. At the evening buffet and dance, the veterans and their families visited the public.

Walter Ritchie was the speaker. He went through all the different stories and all the different places where they had been in action. He noted that *Waskesiu* has been referred to as a lucky ship. Something happened every time that they went out. The guests were very appreciative of the efforts of the people of Waskesiu Lake.

On Sunday morning, a remembrance service in honour of HMCS *Waskesiu* and its crew was held. Participants included the following: Lt.(N) Megan McKenzie, officer of the day; Rev. Rick Burk, Padre NLC W.K. Reed #5; Travis Adema, bugler; Clark Northery, piper; PO1 Jonathan Burk, Bos'n RCSC 118 Rawalpindi; CPO Aaron Burk, quarterdeck (bell) NLC W.K. Reed #5; Cliff Adams, scripture reading (wisdom); John Rickard, scripture reading (gospel); Walter Ritchie, words of celebration; Bruce Menzies, words of remembrance.

The colour guards included Prince Albert Legion Colour Guard, RCMP Colour Guard, HMCS *Unicorn* Colour Guard, and Prince Albert Sea Cadets Colour Guard and Band. Local legion veterans also participated in the service.

After the service, the veterans met the public. Waskesiu Community hosted a luncheon at the Hawood Hotel. Notable were the two large cakes that were decorated with a picture of HMCS *Waskesiu*.

On Sunday evening, Don and Margaret Ravis hosted a reception at their home. The veterans and their families were so appreciative for the time and effort that this couple had put forth to make this weekend memorable . Others who received special mention for their contribution in the planning of activities are Cliff Adams, Dorell Taylor, and a large committee of local citizens.

Waskesiu veterans and wives and children who were able to be in attendance include the following: Cliff and Donna Adams; Gordon Arnold; George and Phyllis Devonshire; Bill Gibb; Claude, June, Mici, and Renée Joyal; Andy Kaija; Bud and Joan Lear; Bruce and Mary Menzies; Herb Parker; John and Carolyn Rickard; Walter and Denise Ritchie; Charlie Robinson; Harry Rushton; Bernard and Margaret Talwin; Dorell Taylor; Al and Alma Tustijan; Roy Venner; Art and Enid Wall; and Ben Webb.

28

Waskesiu Lake, Saskatchewan

In the mid nineteenth century, James Bird shot what he believed to be a moose when he was hunting in the Shady Lake area. When he discovered that it was an elk, he named the huge lake where it lived Red Deer Lake because of the colour of the animal.

In 1927, land in the area was set aside to become a park. J. B. Harkin, Dominion Parks Commissioner, said when he saw the area that it was "a wonderful gateway to the Great North and that the main development to be expected in the park would be summer colonies along the shore of Red Deer Lake."

In 1929, after shifting boundaries, Waskesiu Lake was designated the summer district, *Waskesiu* being the Cree word for "red deer".

By 1930, the basic layout of Prince Albert National Park was in place. Lake Waskesiu, with its sandy beaches, was the focus of activity and the logical place for the townsite.

Since the beach area was to be enjoyed by as many visitors as possible, no residences would be allowed

WASKESIU: Canada's First Frigate

there. It would be a public beach with a campground. This determined the road system to the park.

During the depression, the Canadian government introduced the Unemployment Relief Act to aid those out of work. Federal funds helped finance "work-for-relief" projects. Under Superintendent James A. Wood, camps were set up in the park for men doing relief work.

Because of the programme, many changes to the area occurred. An all-weather highway through the park and other access roads were constructed. Other construction included the following: provisions for recreation and accommodation facilities along the southern shore, the breakwater, a new wharf for tour boats; two bath houses along the beach; the foundation for four tennis courts; the grooming of the first nine holes of the golf course, the clearing for nine more holes, the new registration building, and the museum/community hall. Foundations were dug and timber for a golf course clubhouse, staff quarters, park garage and buildings in the business section were cut.

In 1932, an auto bungalow campground called Waskesiu Bungalows Cabins was constructed; and, in 1938, a second one called Hillcrest Cabins was added. This was in keeping with the federal government's new direction to "auto-tourism".

In 1934, under the Bennett government, more money became available through the Public Works Construction Act. Thus, the relief workers were able to construct eight kitchen shelters, two refrigerator houses in the campground, a band shell, and a new recreation field for the children's playground. They finished the first nine holes of golf and continued work on greens and fairways for the last nine holes.

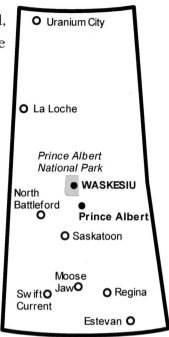

In 1939, the gate at South End, which was to be the gateway into the park on what is now Scenic Highway 263, was constructed.

Because of the changes that had been brought about under the relief program, Superintendent Wood recommended to Ottawa on February 1, 1934, that Waskesiu be the official name of the townsite.

The Waskesiu Lake townsite is located on the east side of Prince Albert National Park, located near the geographical centre of Saskatchewan, about 90 km (56 mi) north of the city of Prince Albert. About 200 residents living there year-round. Over the years, the area has become important as a tourist destination with more than 200,000 visitations to Waskesiu annually.

Waskesiu is a resort community where generations of Saskatchewan families have spent their summers and developed strong bonds with the adjacent lakes and forests. The atmosphere is like an extended family reunion, a safe and exciting place where people find countless ways to celebrate each other and their natural heritage. As "Saskatchewan's playground", the community is a centre for such recreational activities as swimming, fishing, boating, golfing, and hiking.

In May of 2003, the town council passed the proclamation of Freedom of Waskesiu Lake for HMCS Waskesiu veterans.

> Whereas, HMCS *Waskesiu* veterans celebrate the 60th anniversary of their service in the Royal Canadian Navy on board a frigate named after Waskesiu Lake; and
>
> Whereas, the veterans of HMCS *Waskesiu* have an outstanding and distinguished record of service to their country, both in war and peace; and
>
> Whereas, the citizens of Waskesiu Lake wish to extend their gratitude and appreciation to the veterans for the freedom by all of us; and
>
> Whereas, Council deems it appropriate and desirable to honour the HMCS *Waskesiu* veterans on this occasion of their visit to Prince Albert National Park;
>
> Therefore, be it resolved that pursuant to the motion unanimously passed in council on May 16, 2003, the Freedom of Waskesiu Lake be conferred upon HMCS *Waskesiu* Veterans at a special ceremony on June 14, 2003.
>
> Rod Blair
> (Superintendent, Prince Albert National Park)
> Don Ravis
> (Chair, Waskesiu Community Council)

29

Arctic Star

Many survivors of the Murmansk campaign voiced disappointment that there was no official recognition for *Waskesiu*'s service on the Murmansk Run.

The convoys to Murmansk were a vital lifeline for the Russians in their war effort. The Germans were most aware of this and did whatever they could to disrupt it. In this campaign, entire convoys were decimated and almost wiped out in long voyages under a hail of torpedoes, bombs, and shells from U-boats, aircraft, and surface ships.

Ice had to be chipped off the ship so that it would not become top-heavy. Should there be the sinking of a ship, the water was so cold that a sailor could not survive more than five minutes.

They had won the decisive campaign with the war materiel and means to withstand invasion and conquest, and finally to join the Allies in overcoming the Nazi aggression of World War II.

The Russian government first approached the British government in 1985 with a view to offering a commemorative campaign medal, known as "*50 Years Since the Victory in the Great Patriotic War 1941-1945*", in appreciation.

Several proposals were made over the years, but it was only after the end of the Cold War and after conditions were satisfied regarding the award of decorations to British veterans by a foreign government that the British prime minister and his cabinet approved this as acceptable.

As a result, and with the approval of the Queen, on March 7, 2005, British prime minister Tony Blair announced, at a reception for Arctic veterans, the introduction of the new Arctic emblem to be worn as a unique campaign medal. The *Arctic Star* finally became available in the summer of 2006.

After more than fifty years, some of the Canadians were pleasantly surprised to receive a commemorative medal from the Russian government for helping to take much-needed supplies to Russia. Members of *Waskesiu* were awarded both the Russian medal and the British medal.

The *Arctic Star*, a long overdue decoration, recognizes the particular appreciation and honour of the exceptionally heroic Allied Naval and Merchant personnel in their struggle against the freezing cold of the Arctic sea and the violent heat of a determined and dangerous enemy in order to maintain the vital lifeline of war materiel to the USSR.

It is a small, star-shaped white emblem with a red centre, representing the Soviet Union of the time. It was awarded to veterans of the Arctic convoys and families of the men of the Murmansk Run who have passed away.

The push to have a medal to honour participants of this exercise was led by Commander Eddie Grenfell. It was felt that the demands and sacrifices of the Arctic should be recognized as separate from those of the North Atlantic.

Following is the text of a letter from Vitaly Churkin, of the Russian embassy in Ottawa, to Bruce Menzies regarding the medal. Other recipients received similar letters.

> I would like to inform you that in accordance with the decree of the President of the Russian Federation of March 22, 1996, you are awarded with the Russian commemorative medal '50 Years Since the Victory in the Great Patriotic War 1941-1945' in recognition of your service with the famous Arctic convoys to Russia during the Second World War.
>
> I have to mention, however that the Canadian government notified us that 'this medal is not accepted as part of the Canadian Honours System' and that is why it is not for wearing along with other decorations. At the same time we were informed that the Canadian government had no objections to the veterans

keeping the medal '50 Years Since the Victory
in the Great Patriotic War 1941-1945' as a sign
of honour and remembrance.

Please accept the decoration and our
warmest congratulations.

The one sad part of this exercise was that many
crew members of HMCS *Waskesiu* and other ships did
not live long enough to know that they had been
recognized by both the Russian and British
governments.

Afterword

HMCS *Waskesiu* was paid off on January 29, 1946. That same year, her bell was presented to the Prince Albert Historical Museum.

She was sold to the government of India in 1947 for the Kolkata [Calcutta] Port Trust and became the HMIS *Hooghly* in 1950. The frigate that had seen so much wartime action had retired, perhaps fittingly, to a peaceful occupation.

The ship served as a pilot vessel for the Hooghly River from 1950 to 1963. It was from this vessel that pilots used to embark ships that wished to navigate the Hooghly River to the Port of Kolkata. It was frequently anchored off Sandheads, the mouth of the Hooghly River.

After she finished her service in 1963, she was disposed of as scrap.

A

Painting on Front Cover

The painting on the front cover is of K330, HMCS *Waskesiu*, while on patrol.

In 1985, Robert Banks was commissioned by a corporation to paint a picture of HMCS *Waskesiu* to commemorate the 75th anniversary of the Royal Canadian Navy. A copy of the painting hangs in the lobby of the Hawood Hotel in Waskesiu, Saskatchewan.

Robert Banks is an artist who has always welcomed the challenge of painting subjects of a mechanical nature. While he enjoys painting landscapes and seascapes, since childhood he has had a special preference for classic automobiles, locomotives, ships, and aircraft, all of which have featured prominently in his artistic career spanning the last fifty years.

He was born and educated in Vancouver and studied at the Vancouver School of Art and in New York. His work is found in many private and corporate collections in North America and Europe.

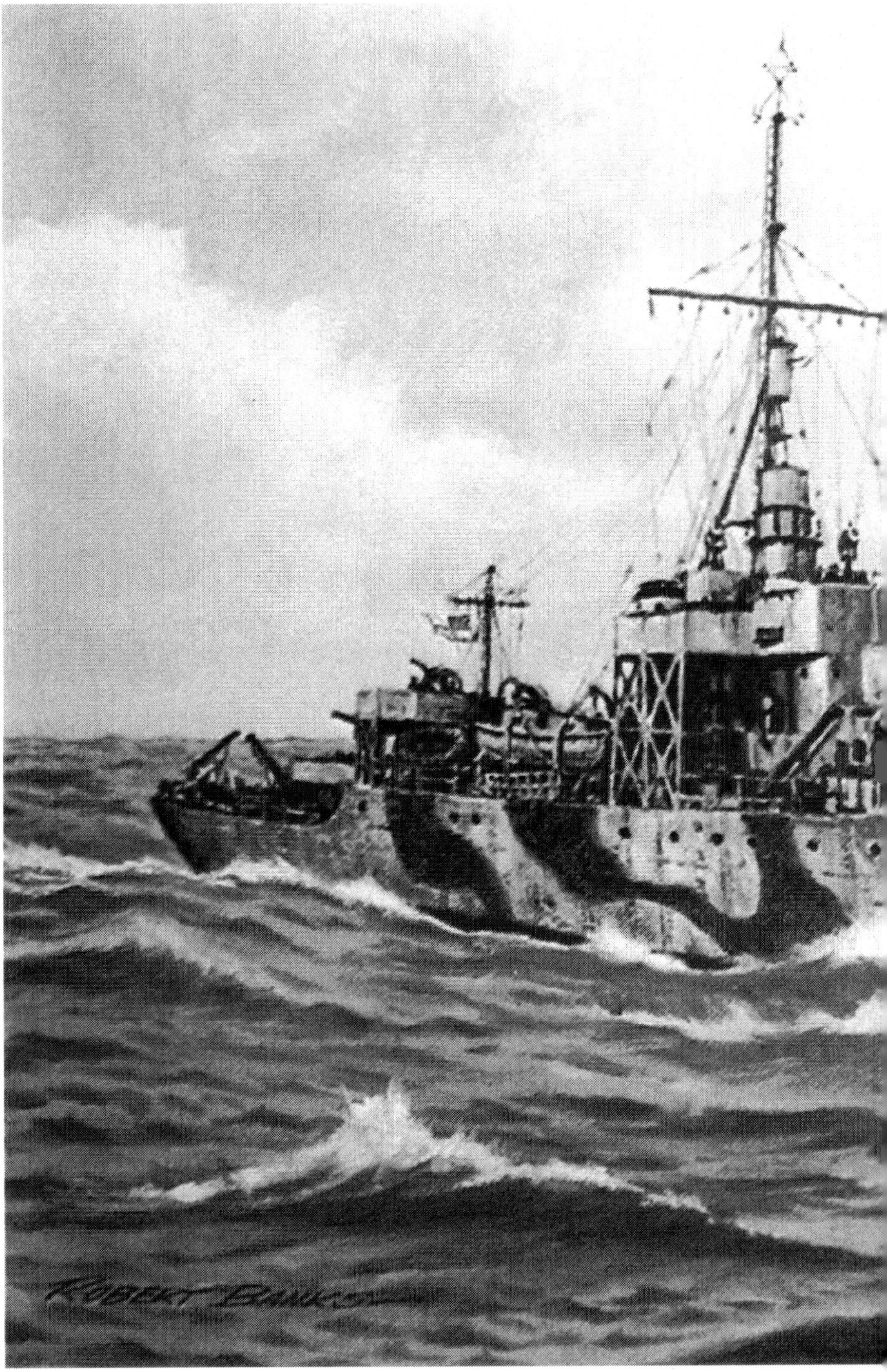

A. Painting on Front Cover

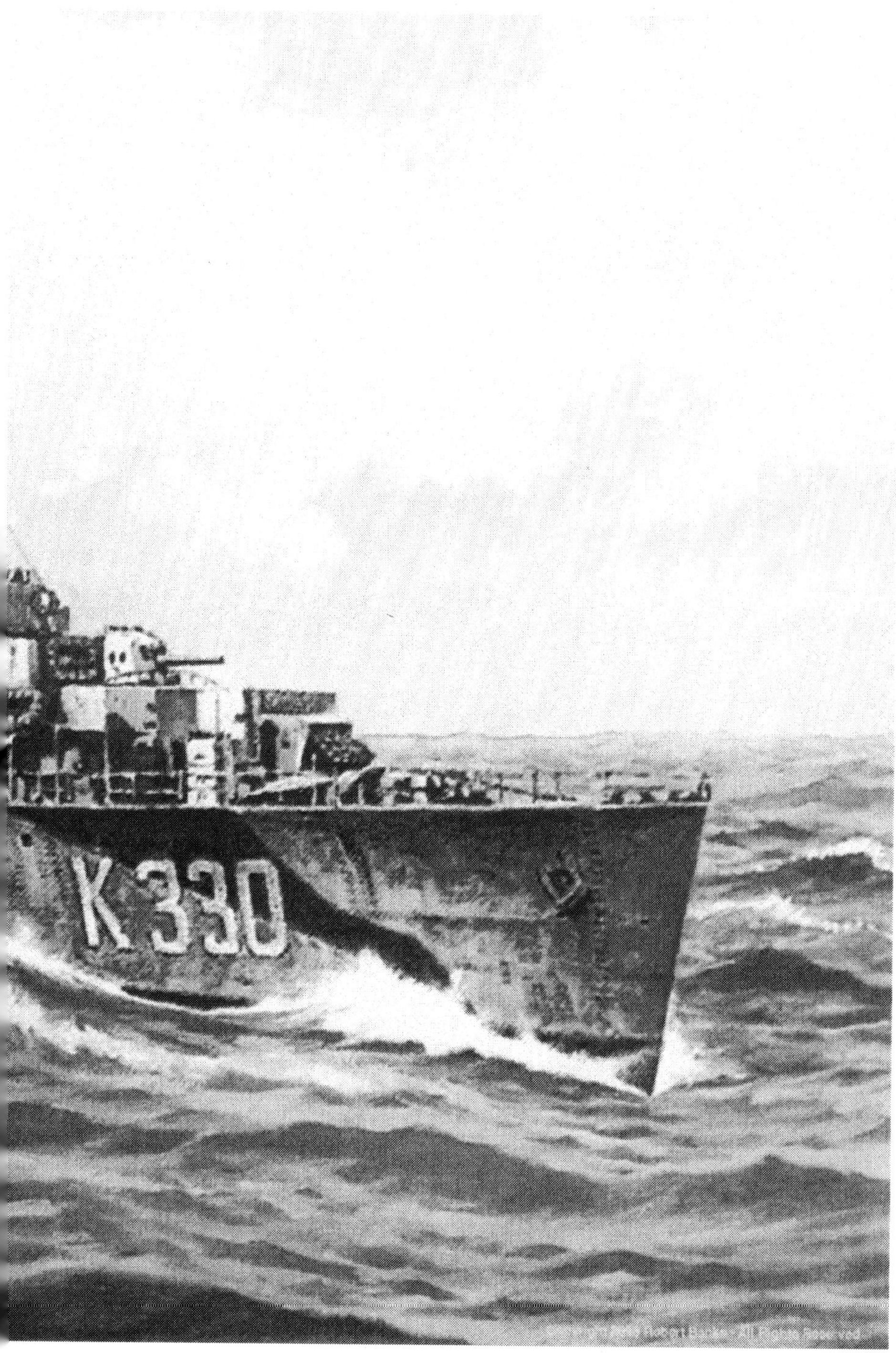
K330

B

Painting on Back Cover

The painting on the back cover is of the sinking of the German submarine U-257 to commemorate the 75th anniversary of the Royal Canadian Navy.

Bo A. M. Hermanson, the artist of this painting, was born in the city of Orebro, Sweden, in 1939. He came to Canada with his parents in 1954, firstly to Toronto. In the summer of 1955, Bo went to sea as a Deck Officer Apprentice in the Swedish cargo liner *Minnesota* of the Transatlantic Steamship Company.

Upon Bo's return to Toronto in the fall, the family moved to West Vancouver, where Bo attended high school and graduated in 1958. In 1962, after graduating from the Art Centre College of Design in Los Angeles, he returned to practise as a design consultant in Vancouver. During the next twenty years, Bo was mainly associated with the firms of E. A. Morrison and Associates and John Hanson Architects.
He started dabbling in marine painting in 1978, and upon moving to Victoria in 1982, began painting in earnest. An early painting of a WWII corvette caught the attention of the navy and resulted in numerous

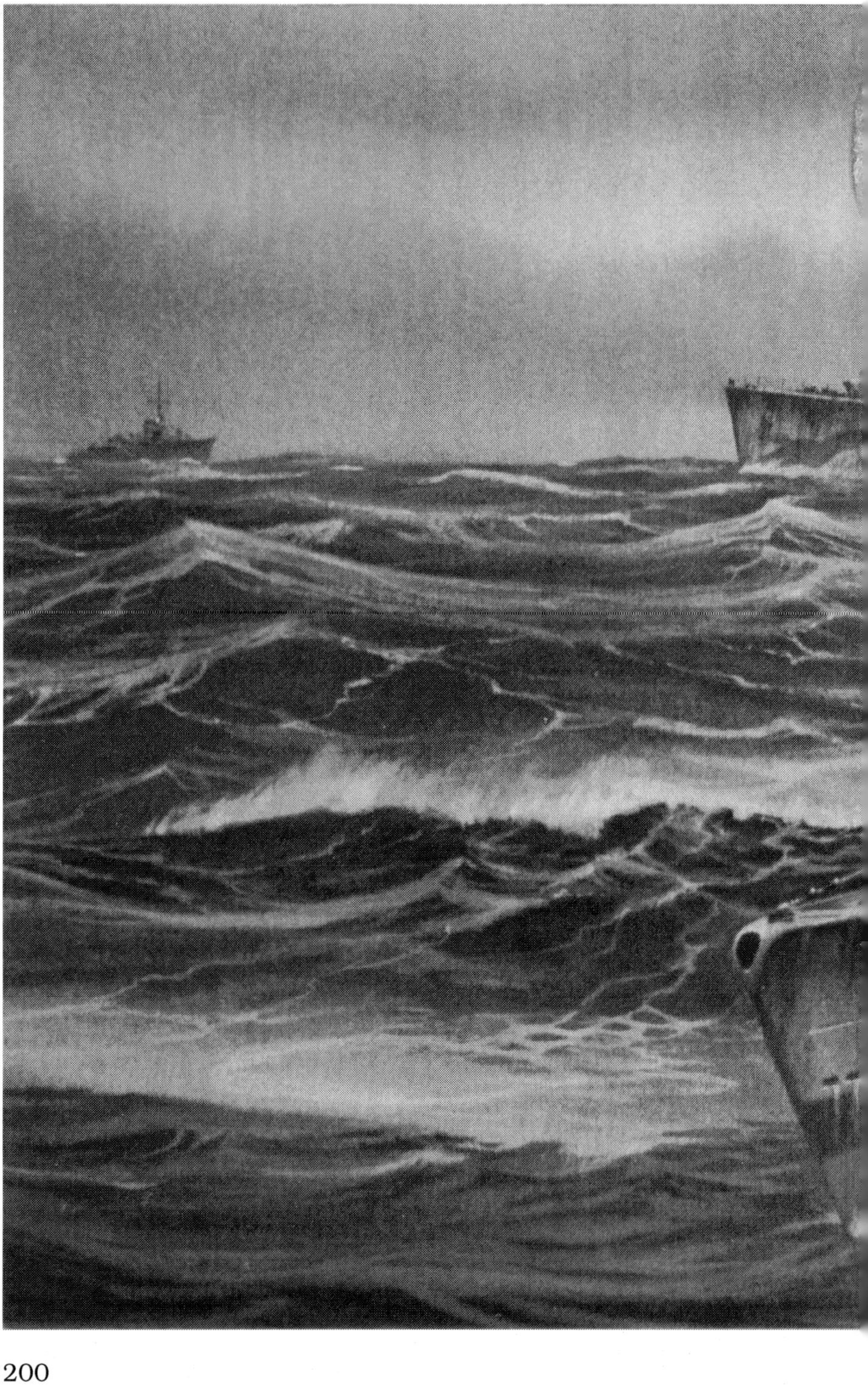

B. Painting on Back Cover

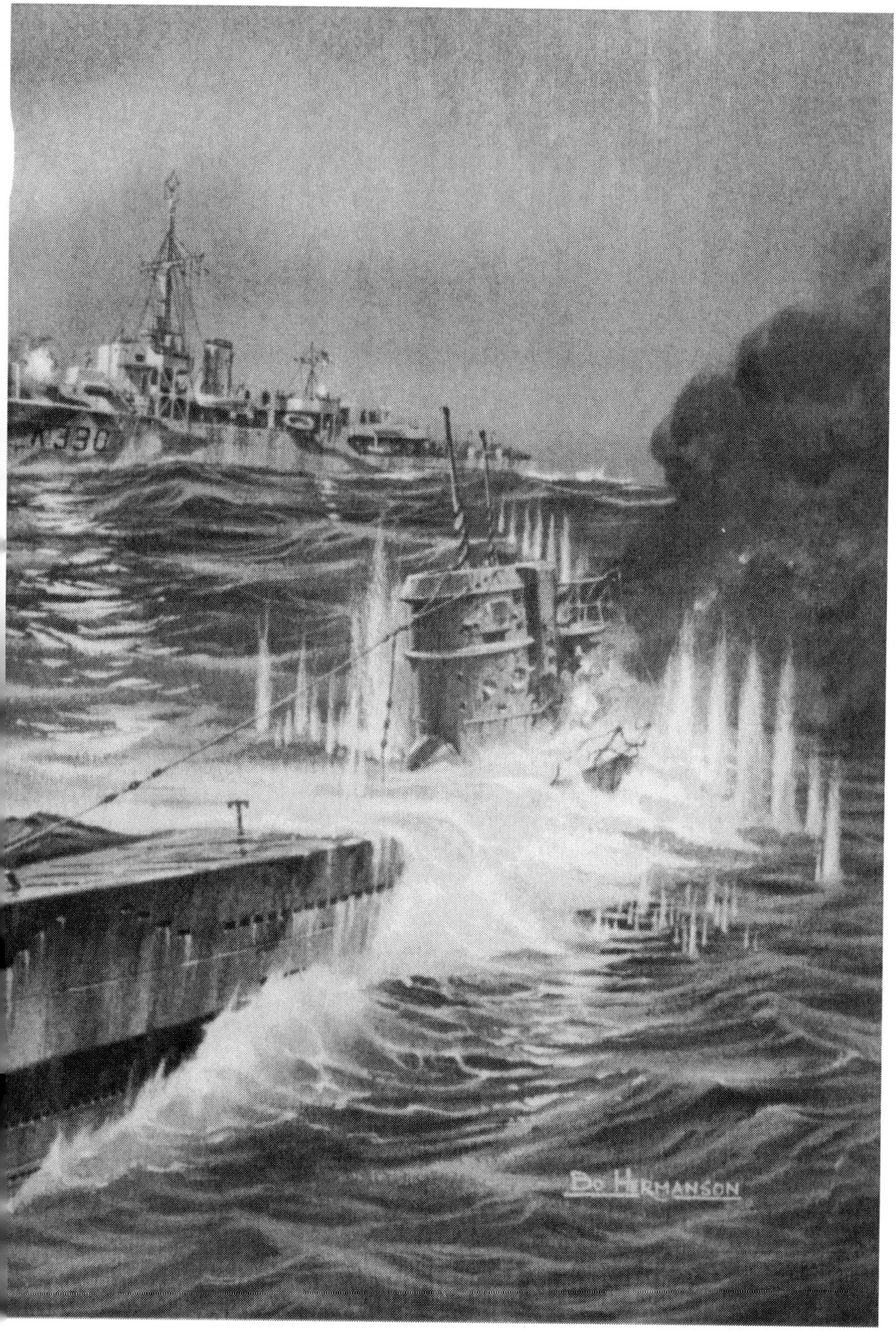
K330
BO HERMANSON

commissions to paint HMC ships on both coasts. Over fifty commissions to paint the ships of Canada's naval forces testify to his popularity in the naval community.

Bo Hermanson's paintings are noted for their great accuracy in the rendition of both ships and their environment, a legacy from his architectural background. His paintings and prints are in collections in Canada, United States, United Kingdom, France, Sweden, Russia, Japan, and South Korea.

Bo has spent well over 500 days at sea with the Canadian Navy, and has sailed in all the types of ships operated by the navy.

He possesses a Bridge Watchkeeping Certificate, is a Naden Wardroom member, and is a member of the Vancouver Island chapter of the Naval Officers Association of Canada. He is also a member of the Canadian Society of Marine Artists. Bo lives with his family and two cats on Glengary Farm in Metchosin, just west of Victoria.

Glossary

AB: Able seaman.

able seaman: Second-lowest non-commissioned rank, above ordinary seaman and below leading seaman, equivalent to private.

ack-ack: Slang for anti-aircraft fire.

action station: Ship alerts given to prepare the crew for battle, equivalent to "general quarters".

aft: Toward the back of the ship.

aircraft carrier: Large warship designed as a seagoing airbase.

Allied: Countries officially opposed to the Axis powers (Germany, Japan, et al.).

artificer: Electro-mechanical specialist.

A/S: Anti-submarine.

ASDIC: Sound detection apparatus derived from Anti-Submarine Division supersonics.

AWOL: Absent without leave.

babbit: Soft metal alloy used to reduce friction in bearings.

banyan: Longstanding naval tradition that provides a break in routine and promotes comradeship among the crew.

barrage gun: Missile launcher that sends a volley of rockets.

battery: Group or unit of guns.

bells: Trousers that become wider below the knees.

bos'n: Boatswain; warrant or petty officer in charge of hull maintenance and deck crew.

bos'n chair: Seat used to suspend a person from a rope.

bos'n pipe: Whistle that changes pitch and used as a signaling device on a ship.

bow: Front end of a ship.

brig: Military prison or jail on a ship.

bulkhead: Wall within the hull of a ship.

buzz bomb: Flying bomb or missile. *(see* **V-1***)*

cat gear: Clanking metal bars attached to a long cable from the stern of the ship to attract acoustic torpedoes away from the ship itself.

chief petty officer: Senior non-commissioned rank, above petty officer and below warrant officer, equivalent to staff or flight sergeant.

CGS: Canadian Government Ship.

CO: Commanding officer.

commander: Commissioned officer, ranking above lieutenant-commander and below captain, equivalent to lieutenant colonel.

commissioned: Ship has been accepted into active service with a crew and commanding officer.

conning tower: Small watertight compartment within a submarine's sail containing the periscopes.

convoy: Group of ships traveling together for mutual support.

corvette: Small, maneuverable, lightly armed warship, smaller than a frigate and larger than a sloop, built for patrol and escort duties.

Coston gun: Type of cannon used for shooting a line from one ship to another.

coxswain: Senior non-commissioned officer in charge of the navigation and steering of a ship.

CPO: Chief petty officer.

crow's nest: Platform structure in the upper part of the mast of a ship that is used as a lookout point.

cruiser: Warship larger than a destroyer but smaller than a battleship whose main role was to attack enemy merchant vessels.

CWAC: Canadian Women's Army Corps.

D-Day: June 6, 1944, the day on which the Invasion of Normandy began.

depth charge: An anti-submarine weapon set to explode at a predetermined depth, intending to damage the target by the shock of explosion near it.

degaussing: Process of decreasing or eliminating an unwanted magnetic field.

destroyer: Fast, long-endurance warship larger than a frigate but smaller than a cruiser intended to escort larger vessels.

displacement: Ship's mass, calculated by the mass of water that the ship displaces while floating.

Distinguished Service Cross: Third level military decoration awarded to officers for gallantry during active operations against the enemy.

Distinguished Service Medal: Third level military decoration awarded to ratings for setting an example of bravery and resource under fire, higher in precedence than Mentioned in Despatches and lower than Distinguished Service Order.

dive bomber: Bomber aircraft that dives directly at its target in order to provide greater accuracy and limit the effectiveness of anti-aircraft fire.

dodger: Canvas cover providing partial protection from harsh weather and seas.

doodlebug: Flying bomb or missile. *(see* **V-1***)*

drydock: A narrow basin that can be flooded and drained, allowing a ship to rest for repairs or construction while on a dry platform.

EG: Escort Group.

escort: Warship assigned to protect merchant ships.

evolutions: Operationally-specific training.

Fairmile: Small military vessel built for harbour defense and submarine chasing, designed by the Fairmile Company in England.

five-charge: Pattern of five explosive charges set to different depths.

fore: Toward the front of the ship.

frigate: Anti-submarine escort warship larger than a corvette but smaller than a destroyer.

gang plank: Portable bridge between a ship and a pier.

Grossadmiral: Grand admiral, highest rank in the German Navy, the same as admiral of the fleet in the British Navy, equivalent to a five-star general.

gun layer: Crew member assigned to point and fire guns.

hands: Members of the crew of a ship.

hardtack: Hard, dry cracker or biscuit.

head: Toilet on board a ship.

Hedgehog: Anti-submarine weapon firing a number of small bombs that exploded on contact.

HF/DF: High frequency direction finder, pronounced Huff-Duff.

HMCS: His (Her) Majesty's Canadian Ship.

HMIS: His (Her) Majesty's Indian Ship.

HMS: His (Her) Majesty's Ship, referring to a British vessel as opposed to one belonging to a Commonwealth nation.

hook: Anchor.

Jerry: Commonly used nickname for a German.

jetty: A wharf or pier extending from the shore.

Kapitanleutnant: Third lowest officer's rank in the German Navy, the same as lieutenant in the Canadian Navy, equivalent to captain in the Army.

Kamerad: German word for friend or comrade.

knot: Unit of speed (one nautical mile per hour) equal to 1.852 km/h or 1.151 mph.

laid down: Construction has started in building a ship.

launched: Ship has been put into water.

leading seaman: Junior non-commissioned rank, above able seaman and below petty officer, equivalent to corporal.

leave: Permission to be away from one's unit.

lieutenant: Commissioned officer, ranking above sub-lieutenant and below lieutenant-commander, equivalent to captain in the Army.

lieutenant-commander: Commissioned officer, ranking above lieutenant and below commander, equivalent to major.

list: Tilting of a ship to either port or starboard.

Lt.: Lieutenant.

Lt.-Cdr.: Lieutenant-Commander.

LCT boat: Landing Craft, Tank; amphibious assault ship for landing tanks on beachheads.

Luftwaffe: German Air Force.

materiel: Military equipment and supplies.

May 24: Victoria Day holiday, often celebrated with fireworks shows.

Mentioned in Despatches: Fourth-level military decoration awarded for gallantry or otherwise commendable service, lower in precedence than Distinguished Service Medal (Cross).

merchant ship: Commercial vessel called upon to deliver military personnel and materiel.

merchantman: Cargo ship.

mess deck: Dining area.

mine: Explosive device placed in water to destroy ships or submarines.

ML: Motor Launch; small military vessel designed for harbour defense.

MV: Motor Vessel.

NLC: Navy League Cadet.

Oerlikon: 20 mm anti-aircraft cannon.

ordinary seaman: Lowest of the non-commissioned ranks, below able seaman, equivalent to private.

paid off: Decommissioned; retired from military service.

periscope: Special tube with prisms which allow for surface observation from the submarine while submerged.

petty officer: Senior non-commissioned rank, above leading seaman and below chief petty officer, equivalent to sergeant.

ping: Pulse of sound in sonar.

PO: Petty officer.

POW: Prisoner of war

port: Left side of a ship.

QR1: Qualified Rating, 1st class.

quarterdeck: Area reserved for ship's officers, guests, and passengers.

ratings: Personnel of non-commissioned ranks.

(in the) rattle: Up on a disciplinary charge; in trouble.

RCMP: Royal Canadian Mounted Police.

RCN: Royal Canadian Navy.

RCNVR: Royal Canadian Naval Volunteer Reserve.

RCSC: Royal Canadian Sea Cadets.

Royal Navy: Sea-going defence forces of the British armed services.

RPM: Revolutions per minute.

rudder: A device used to steer a ship.

Schnorkel: Device that allows a submarine to operate submerged while still taking in air from above the surface.

shilling: Coin worth 12 pence and 1/20 of a pound.

shrapnel: Metal fragments and debris thrown out by an exploding object.

sick bay: Compartment in a ship used for medical purposes.

sloop: Small, specialized convoy-defence warship with anti-aircraft and anti-submarine capability.

sponson: Projection from the side of a ship.

Squid: Anti-submarine mortar weapon which launched depth charges.

star shell: Artillery that uses flares to illuminate the battlefield.

starboard: Right side of a ship.

stern: Back end of a ship.

stevedore: Person who works on a waterfront loading and unloading cargo; longshoreman.

stoker: Crew member who keeps the ship's boilers full of fuel.

submarine: Submersible warship usually armed with torpedoes.

swab: Mop the deck of a ship.

sweep: Search for the presence of mines and remove them.

Swordfish: Torpedo bomber biplane.

ten-charge: Pattern of ten explosive charges set to different depths.

theatre: Large geographic area where conflict occurs.

torpedo: Underwater self-propelled missile.

tot: Daily ration of rum.

tropical uniform: White, light-weight uniforms for use in hotter climates.

tropicalization: Protection of electronic devices on board ships in hot, humid climates.

U-boat: German submarine; derived from the anglicized version of the German word *U-Boot*, itself an abbreviation of *Unterseeboot* (undersea boat).

up spirits: Traditional call mustered by Navy men for their daily issue of rum.

USS: United States Ship.

V-1: Flying bomb or missile called *Vergeltungswaffe*, German for "vengeance weapon"; also known as doodlebug and buzz bomb.

VE-Day: Victory in Europe Day.

vice-admiral: Senior commissioned officer, ranking above rear-admiral and below admiral, equivalent to a three-star general.

wardroom: Officers' mess; dining area for the officers.

watch: Shift work lasting four hours, e.g., 4:00–8:00, 8:00–12:00, 12:00–4:00.

whaler: Type of long, open, oar-powered boat that is relatively narrow and pointed at both ends, enabling it to move either forwards or backwards.

Wrens: Women's Royal Navy Service (WRNS). The Canadian counterpart, Women's Royal Canadian Naval Service (WRCNS), adopted the same name.

yard arm: Long, slender spar slung horizontally from a mast.

yards: Places where boats are repaired or built.

yeoman: Rating with secretarial, clerical, or other administrative duties.

zigzag: Forward-moving pattern alternating from the left and then to the right along a general course.

Resources

"19 Germans Rescued after Sub Polished Off." *Globe and Mail*, April 5, 1944.

Backer, Steve. "Type VII C U-boat." http://www.steelnavy.com/CombatSubsTypeVIIc.htm.

"Belated Recognition." *Navy News*. February 2006.

"Canadian Ships Carry New Name." Hamilton *Spectator*, February 10, 1943.

"Crew of Waskesiu Prayed For U-Boat." Hamilton *Spectator*, April 6, 1944.

Denkhaus, Raymond A. "World War II: Convoy PQ-17." *World War II*, February 1997.

Department of National Defence. "Canadian Naval Centennial - Background Information" http://www.navy.forces.gc.ca/centennial/background/background_e.asp?category=70&title=193.

Devonshire, George. "MV Asbjørn, HMCS Waskesiu 1942-1945." http://timetraces.com/nene/george_devonshire/.

Durrant, Gladys, ed. *Esquimalt's First Seventy-Five Years*. Victoria, BC: Municipality of Esquimalt, 1987.

Fraser, Keith. "We Have Become Friends." *The Province* (Vancouver), November 10, 1999.

Granatstein, J. L., and Desmond Morton. *Bloody Victory: Canadians and the D-Day Campaign 1944*. Toronto: Lester Publishing, 1984.

Helgason, Gudmundur. "Frigate HMCS Waskesiu of the River class." http://www.uboat.net/allies/warships/ship/159.html.

Helgason, Gudmundur. "U-257." http://www.uboat.net /boats/u257.htm.

"HMCS Waskesiu Veterans Remember the Second World War" *Maritime Forces Atlantic Trident*, September 7, 1999.

"HMCS Waskesiu Vets Re-unite." Prince Albert *Daily Herald*, June 16, 2003.

Kingston, Gaylord. "HMCS Waskesiu."

"Londonderry Will See Canadians Gone June 10." *Globe and Mail*, June 2, 1945.

"Many Canadians Make Huge Base Like Home Port." Hamilton *Spectator*, February 24, 1944.

Mason, Jerry. "Interrogation Report." http://www. uboatarchive.net/U-257INT.htm.

Ong, David. "U-Boat Insignia and Emblems - U-244 thru U-257." http://www.uboataces.com/ref-insignia20.shtml.

Taylor, Dorell, ed. *Waskesiu Memories, Volume III*. Victoria, BC: Classic Memoirs, 2003.

"The Battle of the Atlantic." *Vancouver Sun*, April 30, 1999.

Veterans Affairs Canada. "History of the Murmansk Run." http://www.vac-acc.gc.ca/general/sub.cfm? source=feature/murmansk/history.

Weggelaar, Hubertus. "U-boat Crew Lists." http://www. ubootwaffe.net/crews/crews.cgi.

Waiser, Bill. *Saskatchewan Playground: a History of Prince Albert National Park*. Saskatoon, SK: Fifth House, 1989.

"Wartime Struggle Results in Peacetime Friendship." Picton *Gazette*, August 18, 1999.

Wikipedia. http://en.wikipedia.org/.

About the Author

Duane Duff grew up in Elgin County, Ontario. In 1953, he spent a few months in the Royal Canadian Navy.

He took his original teacher training in Winnipeg, Manitoba, in 1950-1951. He obtained a Bachelor of Education degree from University of Alberta in 1967. He was in the teaching profession from 1949 to 1990, teaching in Manitoba, Ontario, Alberta, and Missouri. In Alberta, he was a teacher-librarian and a classroom teacher.

After his retirement, he and Pamela, his wife of forty-four years, have lived in Texas, Nuevo León, Chiapas, and British Columbia. He has volunteered in school and public libraries and at a railroad museum. He now writes books as a pastime on experiences of people.